Book 1

SPELLING SUCCESS

Written By

Jenny Nitert and Debra Salerno

Published By

World Teachers Press®

Published with the permission of R.I.C. Publications Pty. Ltd.

First published by R.I.C. Publications Pty. Ltd., Perth, Western Australia. Revised by Didax Educational Resources.

Printed in the United States of America.

This book is printed on recycled paper.

Order Number 2-5149
ISBN 978-1-58324-076-2

G H I J L 12 11 10 09 08

395 Main Street
Rowley, MA 01969
www.didax.com

Foreword

Spelling Success *is a comprehensive, whole-year program providing you with a solid framework to develop independent spellers.*

The aim of the series is to take students back to basics when learning to spell. Each list has been compiled to support this approach with words from proven contemporary lists. These words were chosen to reflect the students' language abilities, interests and experiences.

Students are encouraged, by way of a focus, to discover for themselves key features, patterns, rules, similarities and differences within each list. The variety of activities accompanying each list provides students with the opportunity to use different strategies to consolidate the focus.

Detailed explanations and program outlines have been provided to ensure maximum use and value of the program. There are dictation sentences for you to incorporate into the regular spelling program.

Evaluation has been made easy by the inclusion of a teacher checklist and student certificates. Space for student self-evaluation has also been incorporated at the conclusion of each list.

Contents

Teachers Notes

Lists One to Ten contain one page each, introducing initial and final sounds. Lists Eleven to Twenty-Five contain two pages each. The first page is designed to give the students as much practice looking at and writing the list words as possible, while the second page is designed as a word building and word study page. An outline of how to best use the pages is shown below.

The **list words** are grouped according to:

- initial sounds;
- phonic groups;
- word families;
- phonic families; or
- commonly used words.

This **focus** is designed to encourage students to look for patterns, similarities, or differences within the list.

Students are also asked to underline the key features – this helps them focus on important parts or features of the list words.

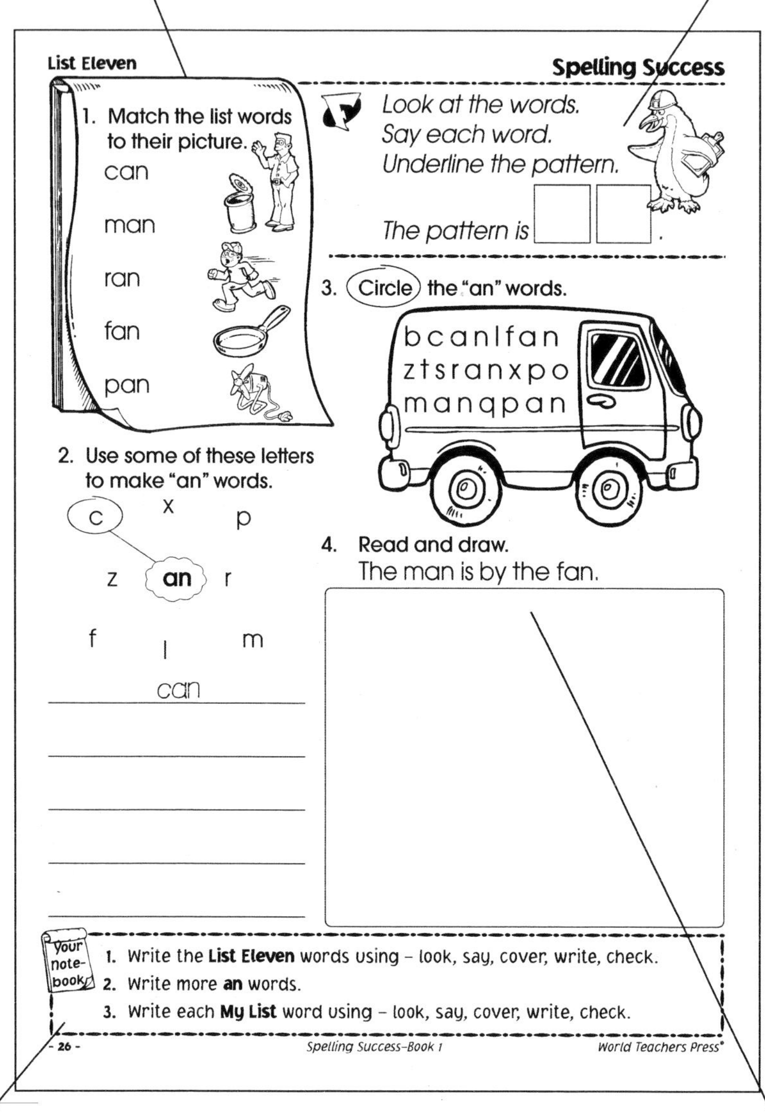

List Eleven

Spelling Success

1. Match the list words to their picture.

can

man

ran

fan

pan

Look at the words.
Say each word.
Underline the pattern.

The pattern is ☐ ☐ .

2. Use some of these letters to make "an" words.

c x p z **an** r f l m

can

3. (Circle) the "an" words.

b c a n l f a n
z t s r a n x p o
m a n q p a n

4. Read and draw.
The man is by the fan.

Your notebook

1. Write the **List Eleven** words using – look, say, cover, write, check.
2. Write more **an** words.
3. Write each **My List** word using – look, say, cover, write, check.

- 26 - Spelling Success–Book 1 World Teachers Press®

Your Notebook activities are designed to be completed over several days in the students' spelling notebooks. The aim is to provide students with several opportunities to write both the list words and their personal list words and to use them in various ways.

These **activities** are designed to provide many opportunities for students to complete or write the list words.

On this page you will find:

- letter chunking;
- read and draw;
- missing letters;
- unjumbles;
- word searches;
- backwards words; or
- rhyming words.

Teachers Notes Continued

The second page is designed to extend and develop students' knowledge and understanding of the word list.

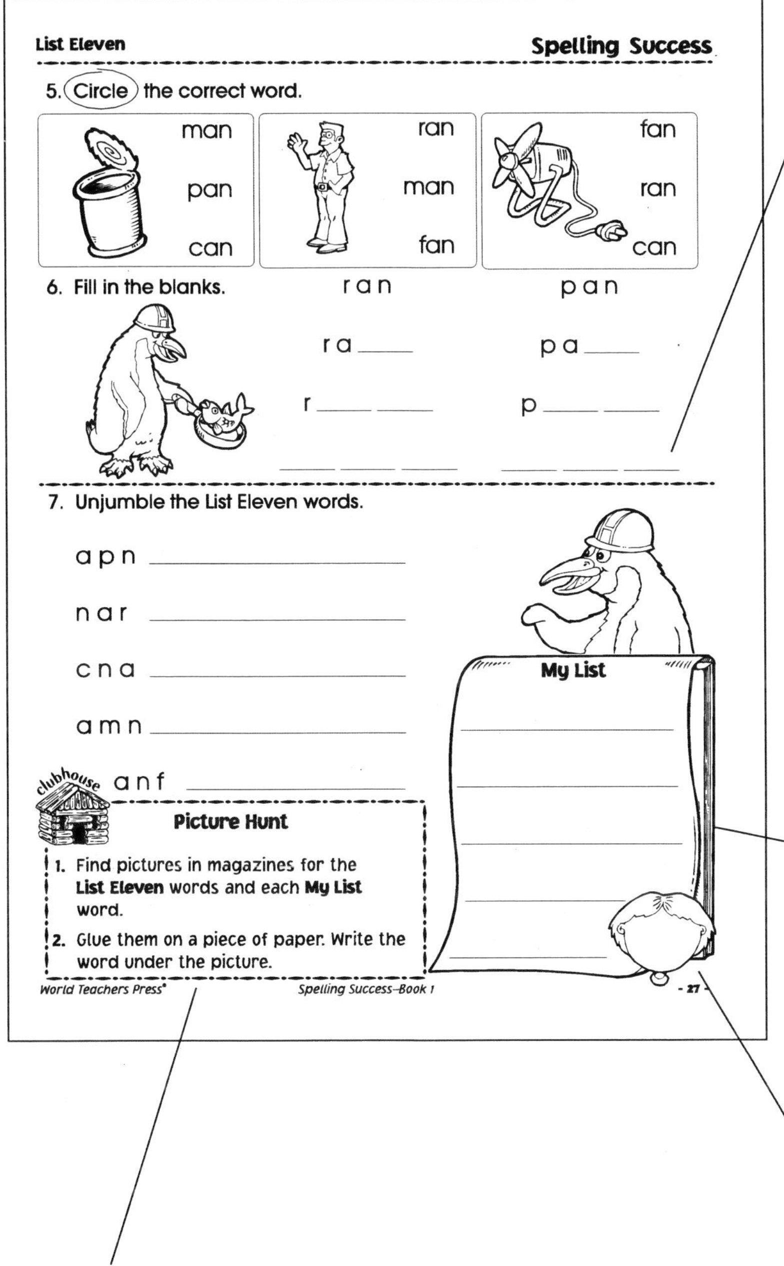

List Eleven — Spelling Success

5. Circle the correct word.

man pan can

ran man fan

fan ran can

6. Fill in the blanks.

r a n — p a n

r a ____ — p a ____

r ____ ____ — p ____ ____

____ ____ ____ — ____ ____ ____

7. Unjumble the List Eleven words.

a p n ____

n a r ____

c n a ____

a m n ____

a n f ____

My List

clubhouse

Picture Hunt

1. Find pictures in magazines for the **List Eleven** words and each **My List** word.
2. Glue them on a piece of paper. Write the word under the picture.

World Teachers Press® — Spelling Success–Book 1 — - 27 -

On this page you will find:

1. **Word Shapes** - encouraging students to recognize the shape of a word to ensure development of visual discrimination.
2. **Word Study** - various activities covering meanings, "Who am I?" and questions to develop understanding of the list words.
3. **Sentences** - allows students to use the words in context to demonstrate understanding of the words.

Students are encouraged to incorporate **personal words** within the spelling program.

These words can be obtained from:

- the students' writing;
- common errors;
- previous spelling errors from list words;
- theme words;
- topic words from science, mathematics, or other subject areas; or
- reading words.

The **face** allows students to evaluate how they feel they handled this list.

The **clubhouse** activities have been incorporated into the book as a form of extension and/or conclusion to the list.

Through an interesting craft activity or game, students are able to consolidate the words from the word list and their own word list.

Suggested Timetable

Lists One to Ten introduce initial sounds and when used with additional activities will take approximately one week. Each list from List Eleven on covers a two-week period and progresses in level of difficulty through the book.

While activities have been provided to consolidate the focus of each list, an eclectic teaching approach is desirable to ensure spelling remains an interesting challenge.

A suggested daily program for the two-week spelling period has been outlined below as a guide to how the program works. These lessons have been developed based on a 25-minute lesson. You may wish to add to or delete from the program according to the time frame that works for your class.

DAY ONE	DAY SIX
• Pretest List One and introduce list words • Encourage students to discover the focus • Underline the key features • Select personal list words and transfer list words to Journal Page (*Journal Page, p14*) • Complete Activity One	• Review the focus for this list • Brainstorm other words that follow the focus • Spelling game or activity *(Spelling Activities, p10–11)*
DAY TWO	**DAY SEVEN**
• Spelling game (*Class or Group Games, p11*) • Review the focus for this list • Complete remaining first page activities • Complete Activity One from *Your Notebook*	• Class Test • Separate the activities on page two - do one per day for the remainder of the program • Spelling game or activity *(Spelling Activities, p10-11)*
DAY THREE	**DAY EIGHT**
• Class Test • Make word shapes for each spelling word and swap with a partner (*Individual Activities, p10*) • Complete Activity Two from *Your Notebook*	• Complete one page two activity • Spelling game or activity *(Spelling Activities, p10-11)*
DAY FOUR	**DAY NINE**
• Make "What am I?" clues for each spelling word and swap with a partner (*Individual Activities, p10*) • Complete any remaining activities in *Your Notebook*	• Class Test • Complete one page two activity • Start *Clubhouse* activity • Dictation sentences *(Dictation Sentences, p9)*
DAY FIVE	**DAY TEN**
• Class Test • Spelling game or activity *(Spelling Activities, p10–11)* • Dictation sentences *(Dictation Sentences, p9)*	• Complete *Clubhouse* activity • Review of list words • Post test

Preparation

A ***Journal Page*** *has been provided on page 14 for photocopying. It is suggested that each student be given a new copy of the Journal Page at the commencement of each new list. This provides the student with a method of recording how he or she is learning the words in each list.*

The ***Clubhouse*** *activities require some preparation, but provided the basics are kept on hand, preparation is kept to a minimum. Some items you will need:*

- flashcards
- glue
- modeling clay
- string
- hole punch
- calculators
- cardboard
- sand/glitter
- scissors
- pipe cleaners
- stapler
- markers/highlighters
- colored/plain paper
- colored pencils/crayons
- grid/graph paper
- coat hangers
- containers of various sizes
- scrap paper

Overview

List	Main Focus	Additional Focus	✓/✗
1	Initial Sounds: **s**, **t** and **b**	Not applicable	
2	Initial Sounds: **a**, **f**, **c** and **e**	Not applicable	
3	Initial Sounds: **r**, **o**, **d** and **i**	Not applicable	
4	Initial Sounds: **h**, **m**, **g** and **n**	Not applicable	
5	Initial Sounds: **w**, **l**, **p** and **j**	Not applicable	
6	Initial Sounds: **u**, **q**, **k** and **v**	Not applicable	
7	Initial Sounds: **x**, **y** and **z**	Not applicable	
8	Review Initial Sounds: **a, e, i, o, u, s, t, b, d, l, m, h, c, k, n**	Not applicable	
9	Final Sounds: **b, f, x, k, s, l, g, t, p, m, d, n**	Not applicable	
10	Final Sounds: **b, d, g, f, m, n, p, l, k, x, t, s**	Not applicable	
11	**-an** family	Correct Word, Fill in the Blanks, Unjumble	
12	**-et** family	Correct Word, Fill in the Blanks, Unjumble	
13	**-in** family	Correct Word, Fill in the Blanks, Unjumble	
14	**-ot** family	Correct Word, Fill in the Blanks, Unjumble	
15	**-ug** family	Correct Word, Fill in the Blanks, Unjumble	
16	Short Medial Vowel Sounds	Word Shapes, Matching	
17	Short Medial Vowel Sounds	Word Shapes, Yes or No Questions	
18	Short Medial Vowel Sounds	Word Shapes, Matching	
19	**-e** family	Sentences, Read and Draw, Homonyms	
20	**-y** family	Sentences, Read and Draw, Add "-ing"	
21	**-ee-** family	Sentences, Body Parts, "Who am I?"	
22	**-oo-** family	Add "-s," Sentences, Definitions, Read and Draw	
23	**-and**, **-end** families	Sentences, Crossword Puzzle, Body Parts	
24	**-all**, **-ook** families	Add "-s," Sentences, Definitions, Book Cover	
25	Commonly Used Words	Sentences, Crossword Puzzle, Read and Draw	

Book One List Words

List Eleven	can, man, ran, fan, pan
List Twelve	vet, met, net, wet, pet
List Thirteen	win, fin, pin, tin, bin
List Fourteen	cot, hot, dot, tot, pot
List Fifteen	hug, rug, jug, mug, bug
List Sixteen	has, ten, big, dog, nut
List Seventeen	had, yes, did, got, bus
List Eighteen	Dad, bed, dig, box, Mom
List Nineteen	be, he, me, we, she
List Twenty	my, fly, by, sky, cry
List Twenty-One	see, meet, feet, need, tree, feed, seed, seen
List Twenty-Two	moon, food, room, soon, boot, roof, zoo, noon
List Twenty-Three	and, hand, sand, land, band, end, bend, send
List Twenty-Four	all, ball, call, small, took, book, look, cook
List Twenty-Five	into, the, him, her, was, get, one, but

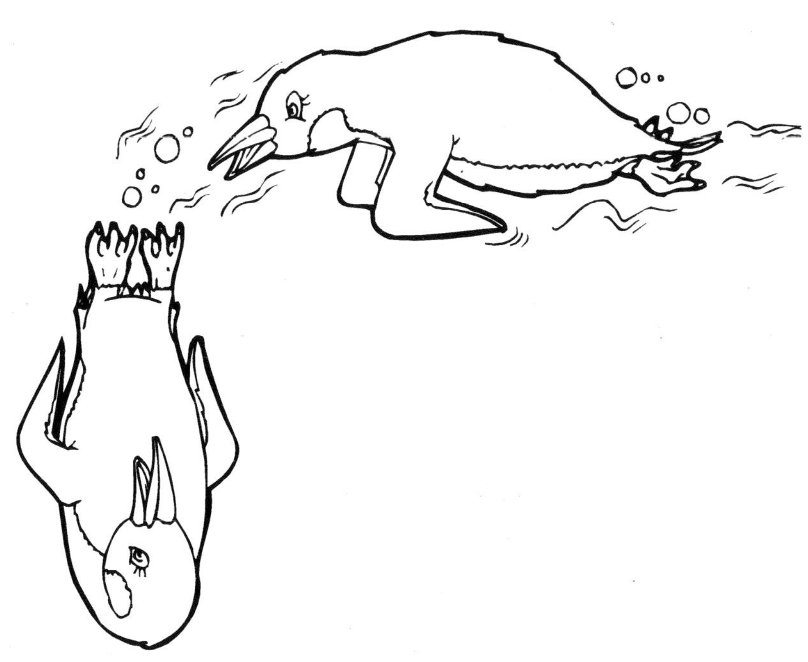

Dictation Sentences

List Eleven

A fan is on.
A pan is by the can.
The man ran to the fan.

List Twelve

The net is wet.
The pet met the vet.
The wet pet ran to the man.

List Thirteen

The man can win.
The pet has a fin.
The pin is in the tin bin.

List Fourteen

The pot is hot.
The tot is on the cot.
It is not hot on the cot.

List Fifteen

It is a tin mug by the jug.
I can hug a bug.
The bug is on the wet rug.

List Sixteen

It is a big bug.
I can pet the dog.
The big dog has a nut.

List Seventeen

Did you hug the dog?
Yes, I did hug the dog.
The man got on the bus.

List Eighteen

Dad is in bed.
Mom can dig.
The pet dog is in the box.

List Nineteen

We can win.
She had a big pet.
He met the vet on the bus.

List Twenty

My dog ran by the bus.
I had a fly on my mug.
My pet can fly and cry.

List Twenty-One

I can see a big bug.
We can meet by the tree.
The feed is in the seed box.

List Twenty-Two

My boot is on the roof.
She can fly to the moon.
Mom met Dad at the zoo at noon.

List Twenty-Three

I had sand in my boot.
We can send a man to the moon.
My pet can land on my hand.

List Twenty-Four

It is a small ball.
I took the book.
We can all look at the cookbook.

List Twenty-Five

I took the book to him.
We all ran into the room.
I had seen her but she had not seen me.

Spelling Activities

The following activities and games have been provided for your use as additional support to the spelling program. They are a guide and can be developed to suit any class, small group, individual student, teaching program, or teaching style.

Choose from the following activities and games if not already covered in the particular list being used.

Individual Activities

Useful for developing familiarity with the list words.

- Make word shapes, word snakes, or word problems for spelling words.
- Find small words hidden in list words.
- Write rhyming words for the spelling words.
- Write the list words in alphabetical order.
- Write spelling words with eyes closed or from memory.
- Sort words according to: initial/final letters, number of letters, number of syllables, number of vowels, number of consonants, parts of speech, or by student's own choice.
- Find antonyms, synonyms, homophones, or homographs for the spelling words.
- Make word builders by adding **s**, **ed**, **ing**, **er**, **est**.
- Rank words from easiest to most difficult to spell or vice versa.
- Write definitions for spelling words.
- Make fold-up books containing spelling words.

Partner Activities

Develops cooperation and increases knowledge of list words.

- Make "What am I?" clues.
- Make an alphabet search.
- Make read and draw activities and swap with a partner.
- Jumble words and swap with a partner.
- Jumble sentences using spelling words and swap with a partner.
- Make simple word searches on graph paper and swap with a partner.
- Make yes/no questions containing spelling words and swap with a partner.

Shared Group Activities

Encourages the exchange of personal list words, therefore, broadening the individual student's word base.

- Make a word bank of words following the same sound or pattern as individuals, partners, small groups, or whole class.
- Put spelling words into sentences – individually or as a whole class.

Spelling Activities Continued

Class or Group Games

Useful for the reinforcement of the list words in a less formal approach.

- Hold simple class spelling competitions.
- Use individual books, charts, shared stories, or poems to find a particular spelling pattern or rule being studied.
- Play concentration, fish, or word bingo.
- Play tic tac toe using visual patterns or sound patterns to match words.
- Play hangman or a similar game where students need to guess the letters in the word.
- Guess my word – students ask questions that require a yes/no response to guess the mystery spelling word.

Clubhouse Activities

Useful for the reinforcement of the list words in a less formal approach.

- Make and illustrate booklets.
- Make bookmarks with spelling words.
- Make word mobiles.
- Make modeling clay or pipe cleaner spelling words.
- Make sand or glitter spelling words.
- Paint spelling words.
- Write spelling words in the shape of a list word.
- Do a magazine hunt for spelling words.
- Trace spelling words on partner's back – partner guesses which spelling word was traced.
- Use bright colors to trace spelling words.

Word Study

A range of blackline masters published by World Teachers Press® are available to support the word study component of this spelling program.

Evaluation Suggestions

Evaluation for each list begins with a pretest of the list words before the students see the list words. This can be used as a benchmark for how well the students learn the list or which words they need to focus on throughout the two-week program.

If appropriate, students can then complete a partner test each day and record their results on their Journal Page. If not, students can be tested every other day by you as a whole class.

A post test is then required at the conclusion of the two-week program to evaluate the students' progress. Problem words are recorded and transferred, ready for their personal lists in the next list of words to be studied.

It is recommended that review tests are incorporated into the program on a regular basis to ensure previous list words are kept current in the students' memories.

Two recording formats have been included. Format one allows for the recording of each test each student takes, while format two allows for easy recording and follow-up of individual words in each list. This allows for flexibility and accountability within the spelling program. It also allows you to easily evaluate each student or the whole class on two different levels of achievement.

Test Checklist   List ____________   List ____________

Student Name	Pre test	T1	T2	T3	T4	Post test	Pre test	T1	T2	T3	T4	Post test	Review

Spelling Matrix

List ______________

Student Name / Words								

Journal Page

List ____________________

How you can become a better speller…

1. **Write it!**
   Write the word on a piece of paper.
   Does it look right?
   If it doesn't look right, try spelling it another way.
2. **Look around your classroom.**
   There are probably many words around you that you just didn't notice.
3. **Ask the teacher.**
   If you have tried the first two, then ask your teacher for help.

Word	Features	T1	T2	T3	T4	T5

CONGRATULATIONS

Spelling Award

____

for ______________________________

____

____

Signed ______________________ Date ____________

Color the pictures that begin with "s."

Circle the beginning sound.

s t b

Color the pictures that begin with "t."

Circle the beginning sound.

s t b

Color the pictures that begin with "b."

Circle the beginning sound.

s t b

Color the pictures that begin with "a."

Circle the beginning sound.

a f

c e

Color the pictures that begin with "f."

Circle the beginning sound.

a f

c e

Color the pictures that begin with "c."

Circle the beginning sound.

a f

c e

Color the pictures that begin with "e."

Circle the beginning sound.

a f

c e

Color the pictures that begin with "r."

Circle the beginning sound.

r o

d i

Color the pictures that begin with "o."

Circle the beginning sound.

r o

d i

Color the pictures that begin with "d."

Circle the beginning sound.

r o

d i

Color the pictures that begin with "i."

Circle the beginning sound.

r o

d i

Color the pictures that begin with "h."

Circle the beginning sound.

h m

g n

Color the pictures that begin with "m."

Circle the beginning sound.

h m

g n

Color the pictures that begin with "g."

Circle the beginning sound.

h m

g n

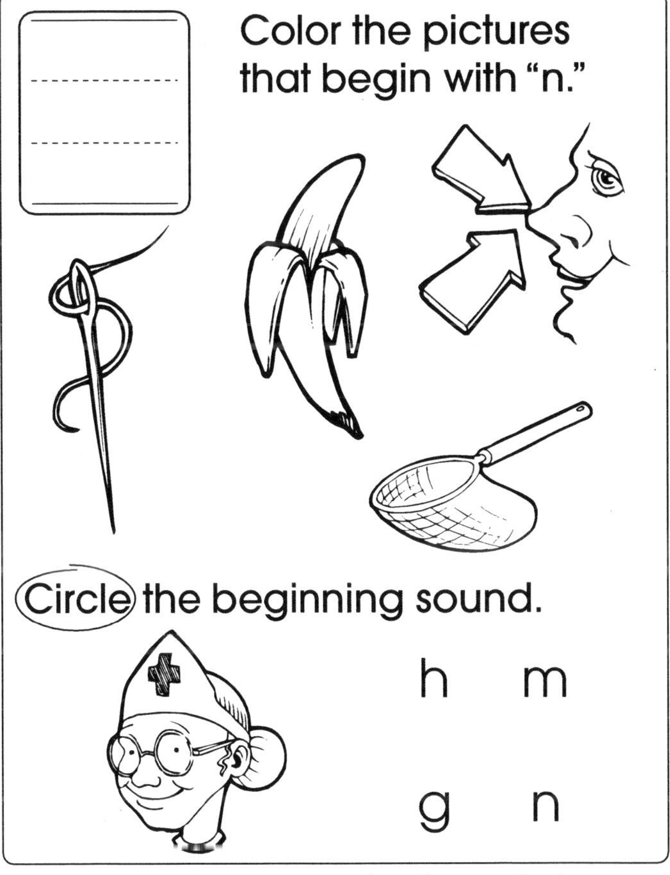

Color the pictures that begin with "n."

Circle the beginning sound.

h m

g n

Color the pictures that begin with "w."

Circle the beginning sound.

w l

p j

Color the pictures that begin with "l."

Circle the beginning sound.

w l

p j

Color the pictures that begin with "p."

Circle the beginning sound.

w l

p j

Color the pictures that begin with "j."

Circle the beginning sound.

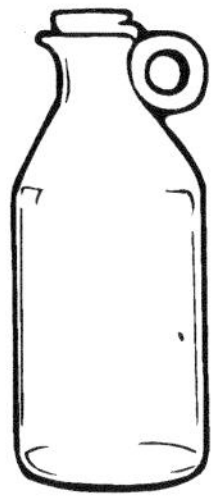

w l

p j

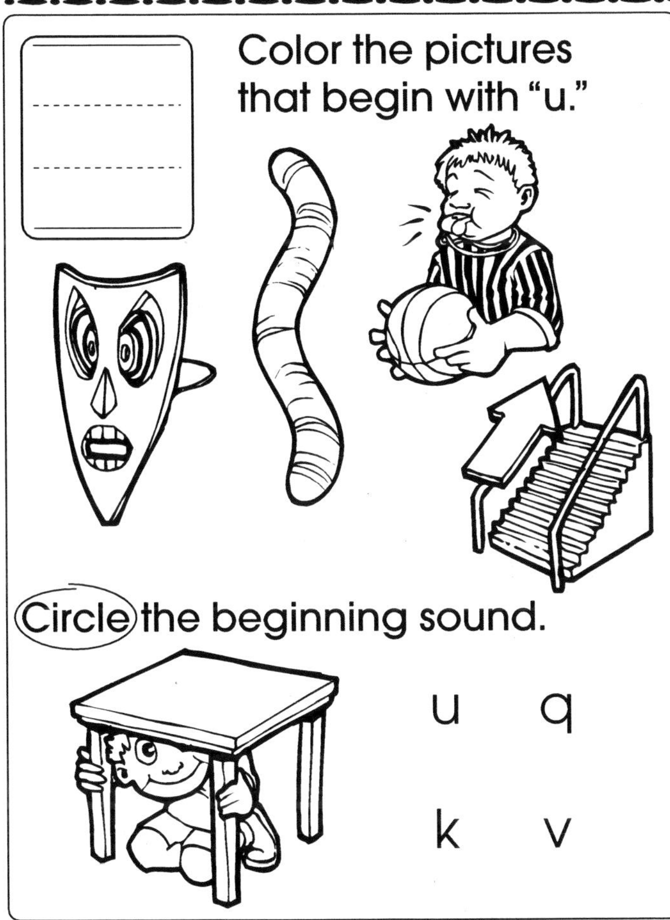

Color the pictures that begin with "u."

Circle the beginning sound.

u q

k v

Color the pictures that begin with "q."

Circle the beginning sound.

u q

k v

Color the pictures that begin with "k."

Circle the beginning sound.

u q

k v

Color the pictures that begin with "v."

Circle the beginning sound.

u q

k v

Color the picture that begins with "x."

Circle the beginning sound.

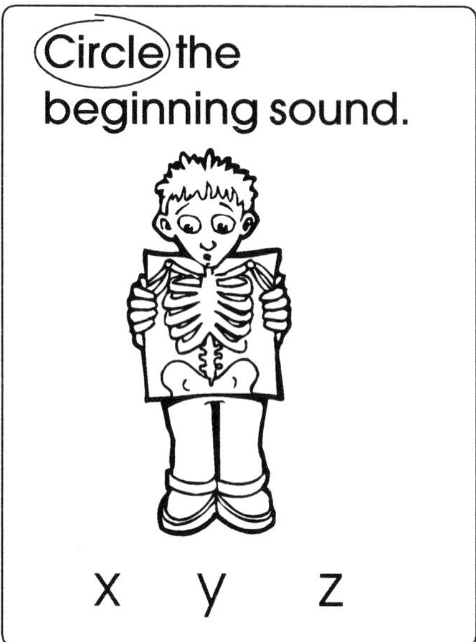

x y z

Color the pictures that begin with "y."

Circle the beginning sound.

x y z

Color the pictures that begin with "z."

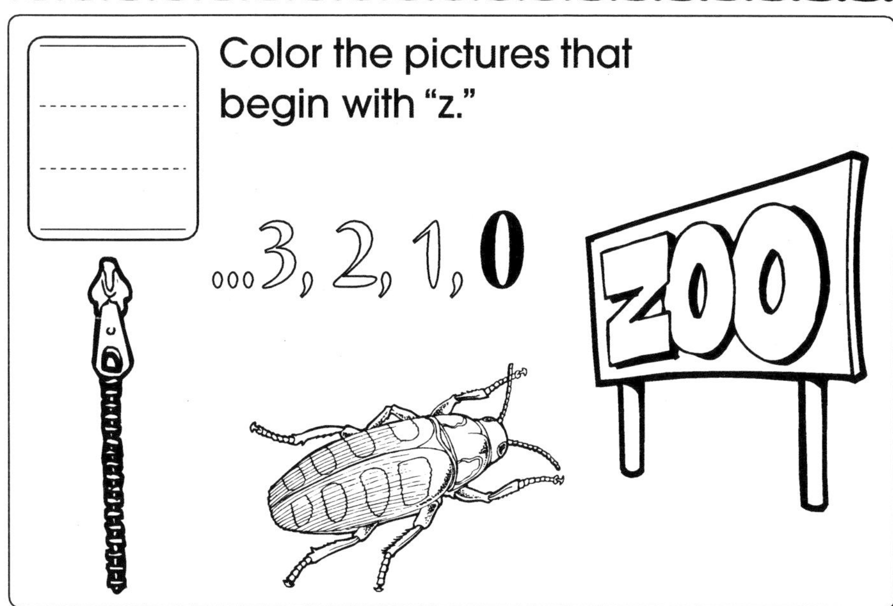

Circle the beginning sound.

x y z

Write the beginning sound for each picture. Color the pictures.

Circle the end sound for each picture. Color the pictures.

Write the end sound for each picture. Color the pictures.

1. Match the list words to their picture.

can

man

ran

fan

pan

Look at the words.
Say each word.
Underline the pattern.

The pattern is ☐☐.

3. Circle the "an" words.

2. Use some of these letters to make "an" words.

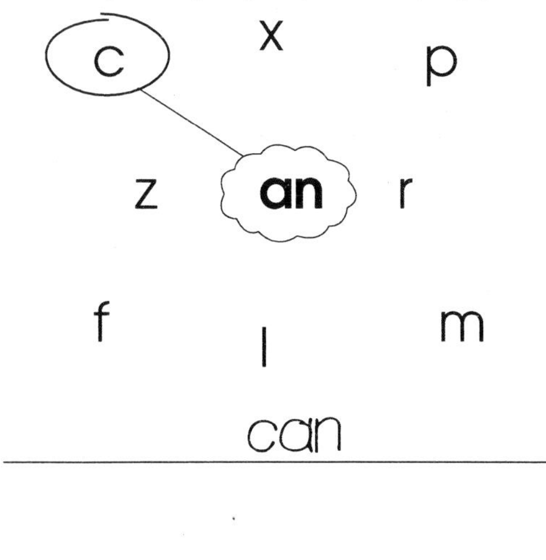

____

____

____

____

4. Read and draw.
The man is by the fan.

your note-book

1. Write the **List Eleven** words using – look, say, cover, write, check.
2. Write more **an** words.
3. Write each **My List** word using – look, say, cover, write, check.

5. Circle the correct word.

 man pan can	 ran man fan	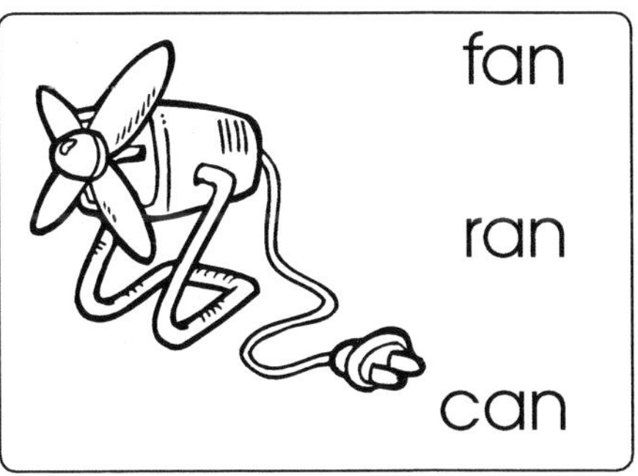 fan ran can

6. Fill in the blanks.

r a n

r a ____

r ____ ____

____ ____ ____

p a n

p a ____

p ____ ____

____ ____ ____

7. Unjumble the List Eleven words.

a p n ______________________

n a r ______________________

c n a ______________________

a m n ______________________

a n f ______________________

My List

____

____

____

____

____

clubhouse

Picture Hunt

1. Find pictures in magazines for the **List Eleven** words and each **My List** word.
2. Glue them on a piece of paper. Write the word under the picture.

Look at the words.
Say each word.
Underline the pattern.

The pattern is ☐☐ .

2. Which word does not have a picture?

____

4. Use some of these letters to make "et" words.

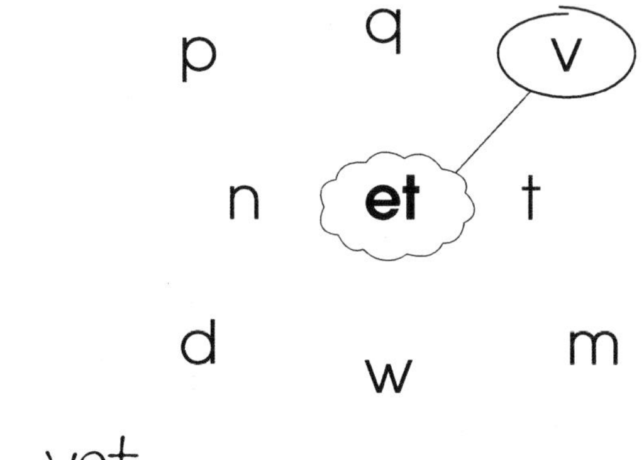

vet _______________ _______________

_______________ _______________

____

3. Circle the "et" words.

5. Color the list words in this picture.

Your note-book

1. Write the **List Twelve** words using – look, say, cover, write, check.
2. Write more **et** words.
3. Write each **My List** word using – look, say, cover, write, check.

6. Circle the correct word.

pet
met
net

vet
pet
wet

met
wet
vet

7. Fill in the blanks.

p e t

p e ____

p ____ ____

____ ____ ____

m e t

m e ____

m ____ ____

____ ____ ____

8. Unjumble the List Twelve words.

e p t ______________________

t e n ______________________

e t v ______________________

t m e ______________________

w t e ______________________

clubhouse

Sand Words

1. Collect pieces of thick cardboard.
2. Use glue to write the **List Twelve** words and each **My List** word.
3. Sprinkle with sand. Press the sand. Shake the card gently.

1. Match the list words to their picture.

win

fin

pin

tin

bin

Look at the words.
Say each word.
Underline the pattern.

The pattern is 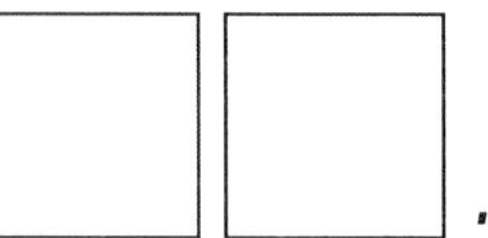 .

3. Circle the "in" words.

2. Use some of these letters to make "in" words.

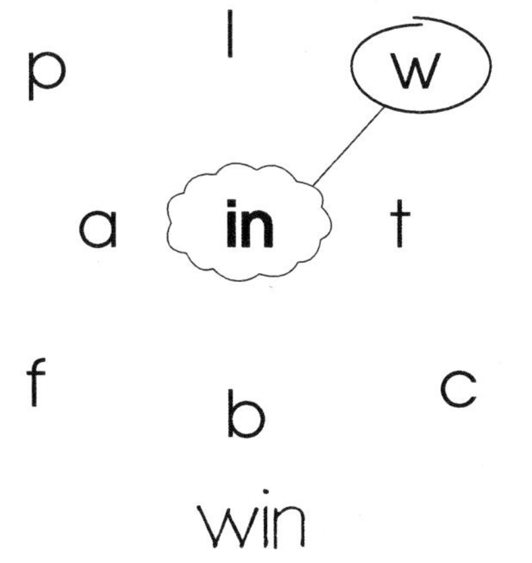

win

---

4. Finish this picture by drawing a fin, a bin and you winning a race.

Your notebook

1. Write the **List Thirteen** words using – look, say, cover, write, check.
2. Write more **in** words.
3. Write each **My List** word using – look, say, cover, write, check.

5. Circle the correct word.

win

fin

bin

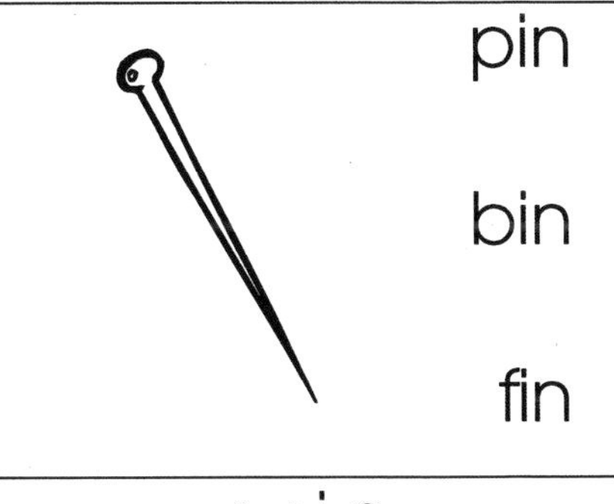

pin

bin

fin

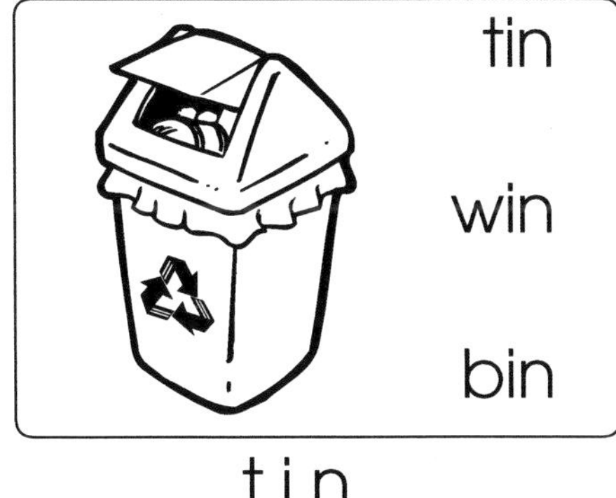

tin

win

bin

6. Fill in the blanks.

w i n	t i n
w i ____	t i ____
w ____ ____	t ____ ____
____ ____ ____	____ ____ ____

7. Unjumble the List Thirteen words.

n i b ____________________

t n i ____________________

w n i ____________________

n i f ____________________

n p i ____________________

clubhouse

Word Ladder

1. Collect blank flashcards.
2. Write a spelling word on each card.
3. Join the cards with string to make a word ladder.

pin

fin

win

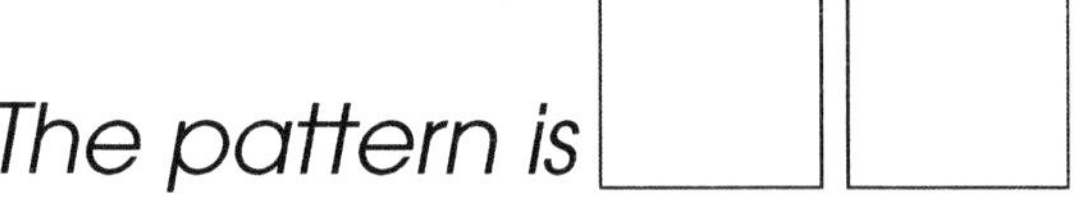

Look at the words.
Say each word.
Underline the pattern.

The pattern is [ ] [ ] .

2. Use some of these letters to make "ot" words.

d a c

s **ot** w

t p h

cot

____

____

____

____

____

3. Circle the "ot" words.

4. Read and draw.
A tot on a yellow cot.

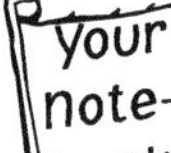

1. Write the **List Fourteen** words using – look, say, cover, write, check.
2. Write more **ot** words.
3. Write each **My List** word using – look, say, cover, write, check.

5. Circle the correct word.

cot
dot
pot

hot
tot
cot

dot
pot
hot

6. Fill in the blanks.

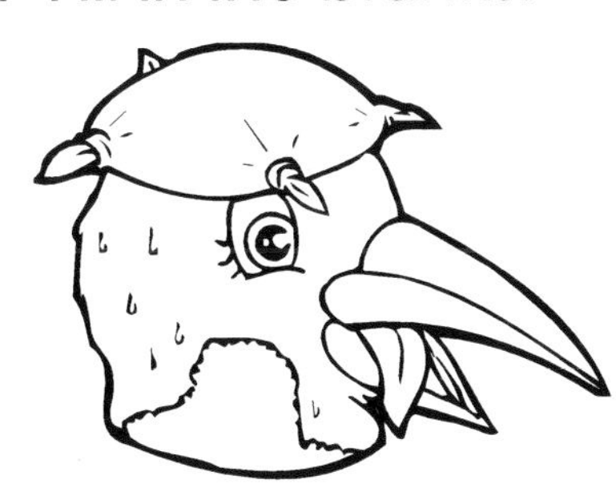

h o t	d o t
h o ____	d o ____
h ____ ____	d ____ ____
____ ____ ____	____ ____ ____

7. Unjumble the List Fourteen words.

o t t ____________________

t p o ____________________

o d t ____________________

t o c ____________________

o h t ____________________

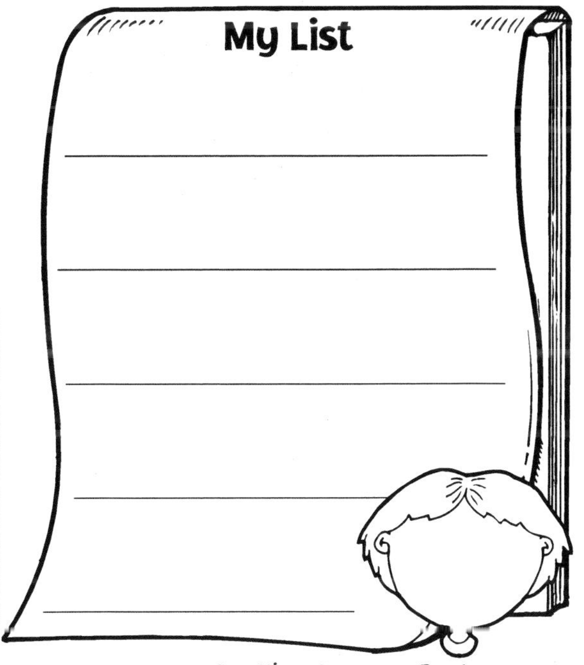

clubhouse

Paint Your Words

Use paint to write the **List Fourteen** words and each **My List** word on thick cardboard.

1. Match the list words to their picture.

hug

rug

jug

mug

bug

Look at the words.
Say each word.
Underline the pattern.

The pattern is 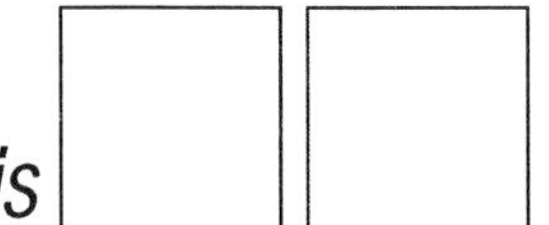 .

2. Use some of these letters to make "ug" words.

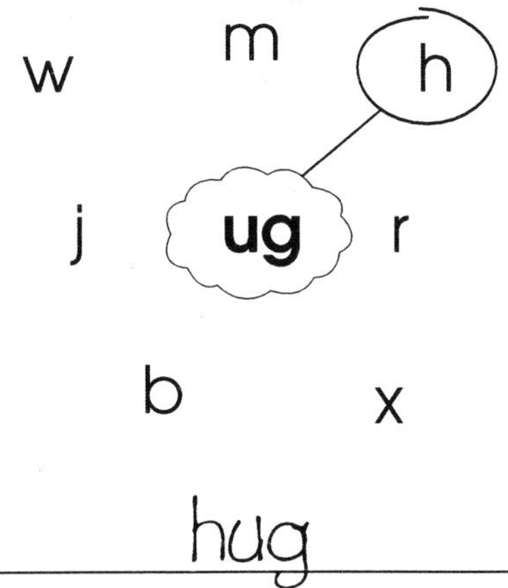

3. Circle the "ug" words.

4. Color the list words in this picture.

Your notebook

1. Write the **List Fifteen** words using – look, say, cover, write, check.
2. Write more **ug** words.
3. Write each **My List** word using – look, say, cover, write, check.

5. Circle the correct word.

hug

jug

bug

rug

mug

hug

jug

bug

rug

6. Fill in the blanks.

h u g

h u ____

h ____ ____

____ ____ ____

m u g

m u ____

m ____ ____

____ ____ ____

7. Unjumble the List Fifteen words.

u r g ____________________

m g u ____________________

g u h ____________________

u j g ____________________

g b u ____________________

clubhouse

Modeling Clay Words

Use modeling clay to make the **List Fifteen** words and each **My List** word.

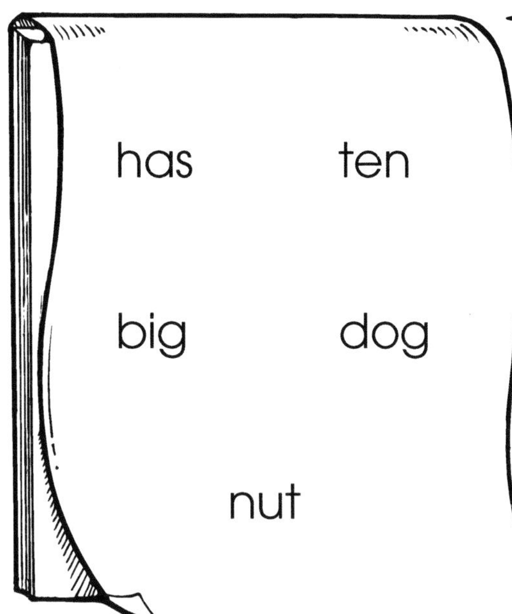

Look at the words.
Say each word slowly.
Listen carefully to each sound.
Underline the vowels.

1. Make the list words using these word parts.

has

2. Fill in the missing letter.

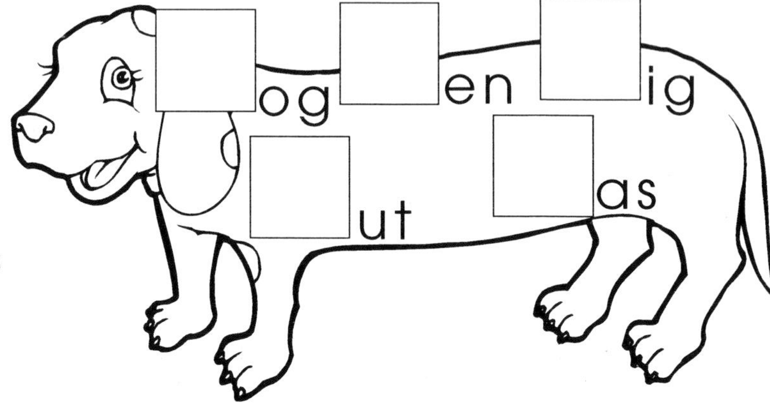

3. Unjumble the list words.

g d o ____________

n e t ____________

a s h ____________

i b g ____________

t u n ____________

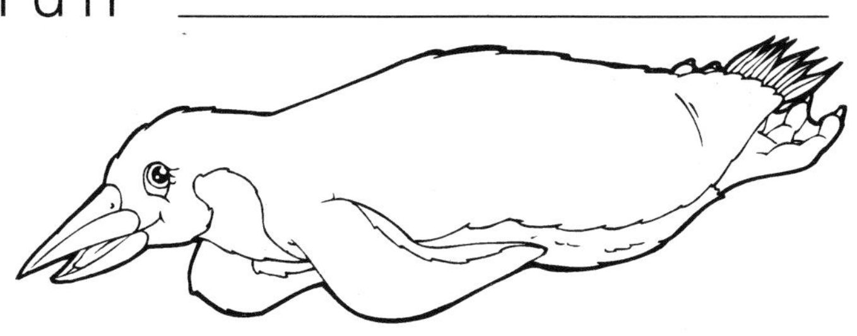

1. Write the **List Sixteen** words using – look, say, cover, write, check.
2. Write two rhyming words for ten, big, dog and nut.
3. Write each **My List** word using – look, say, cover, write, check.

4. Fill in these word shapes.

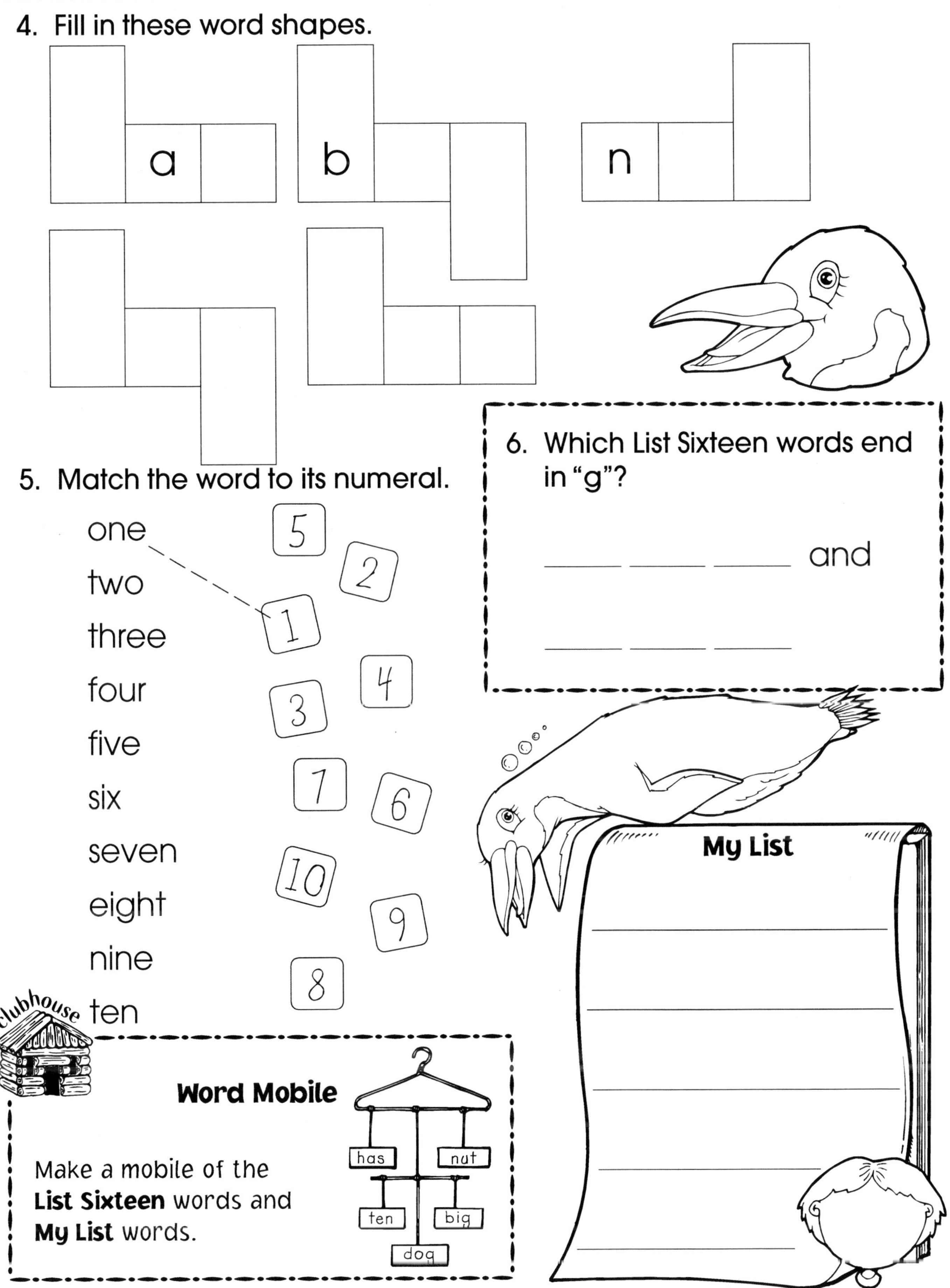

5. Match the word to its numeral.

one
two
three
four
five
six
seven
eight
nine
ten

6. Which List Sixteen words end in "g"?

___ ___ ___ and

___ ___ ___

clubhouse

Word Mobile

Make a mobile of the **List Sixteen** words and **My List** words.

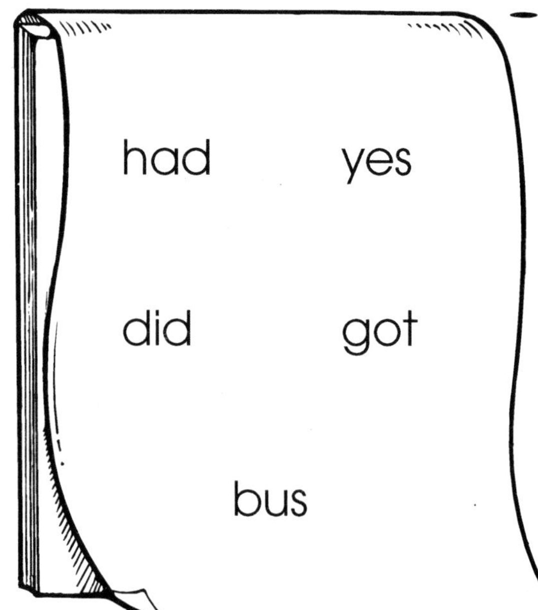

Look at the words.
Say each word slowly.
Listen carefully to each sound.
Underline the vowels.

1. Make the list words using these word parts.

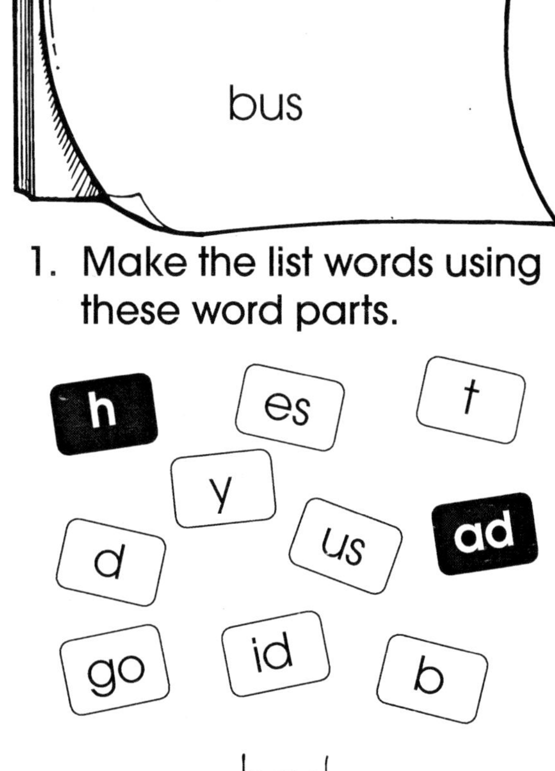

had

____

____

____

____

2. Fill in the missing letter.

3. Unjumble the list words.

s e y ______________________

o t g ______________________

d a h ______________________

s u b ______________________

d d i ______________________

Your notebook
1. Write the **List Seventeen** words using – look, say, cover, write, check.
2. Write two rhyming words for had, did and got.
3. Write each **My List** word using – look, say, cover, write, check.

4. Fill in these word shapes.

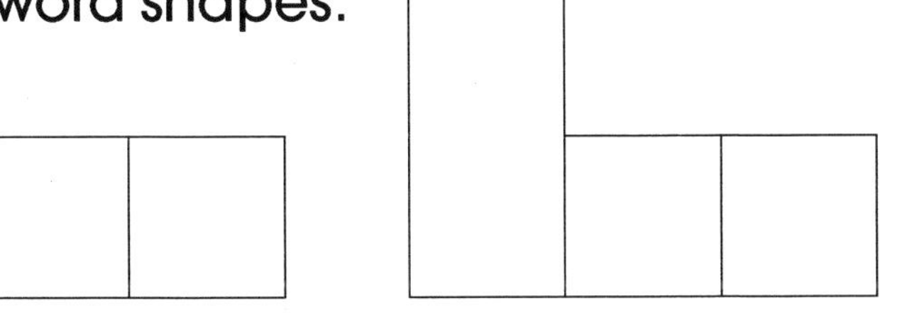

d

5. Which list words end with "d"?

____ ____ ____ and ____ ____ ____

6. Answer yes or no.

Do you like fries? ________

Is it hot? ________

Is an ant big? ________

Can you swim? ________

Do you have a pet? ________

My List

clubhouse

Make a Jigsaw Puzzle

1. Collect blank flashcards.
2. Write a spelling word on each card.

3. Cut each card into a jigsaw puzzle.

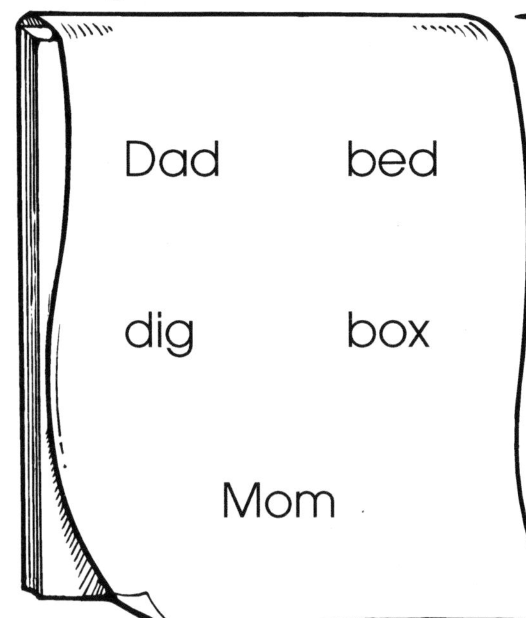

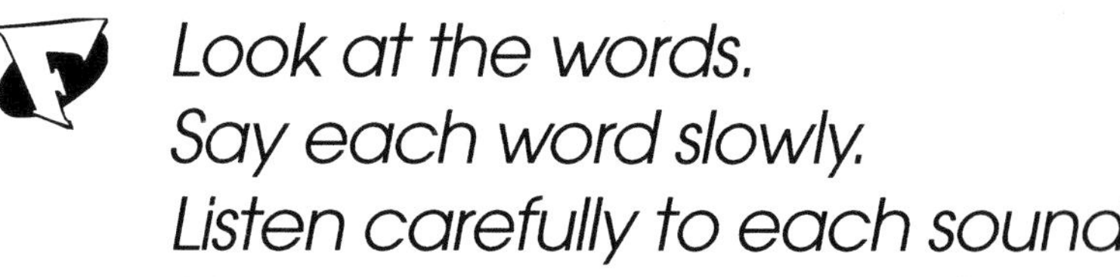

1. Make the list words using these word parts.

Dad

____

____

____

____

2. Fill in the missing letter.

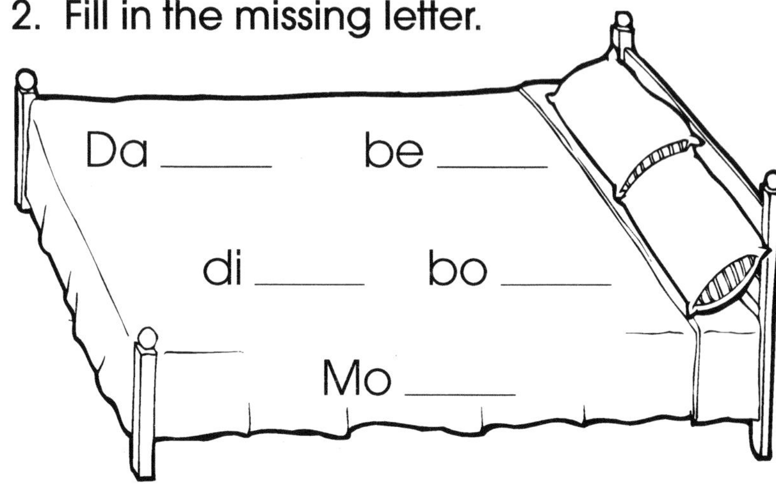

3. Unjumble the list words.

d e b ____________________

x b o ____________________

a d D ____________________

m M o ____________________

g i d ____________________

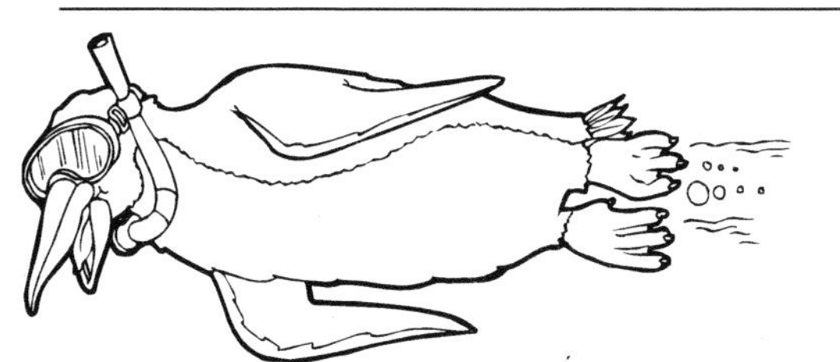

1. Write the **List Eighteen** words using – look, say, cover, write, check.
2. Write two rhyming words for Dad, bed, dig and box.
3. Write each **My List** word using – look, say, cover, write, check.

4. Fill in these word shapes.

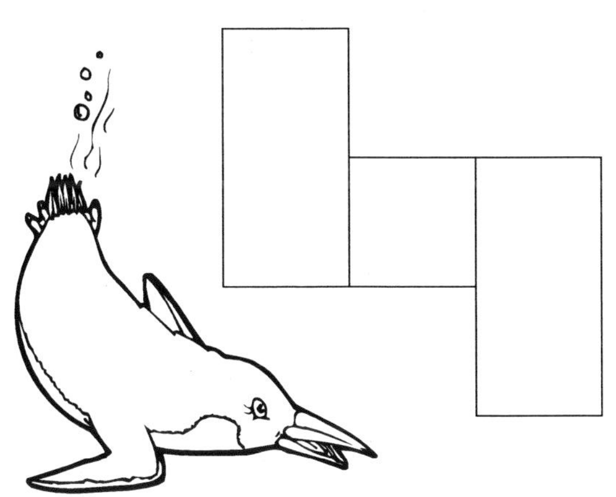

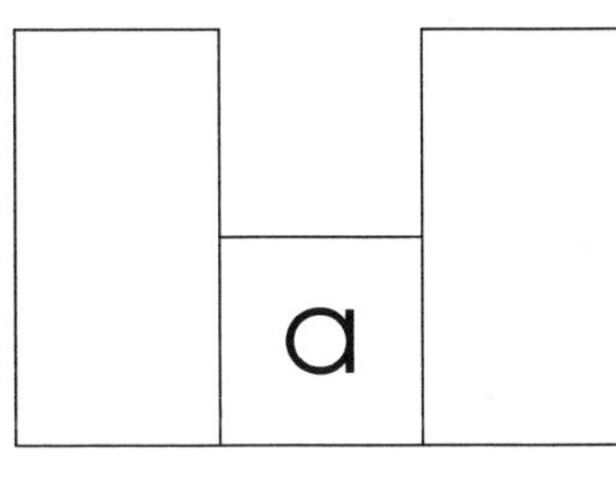

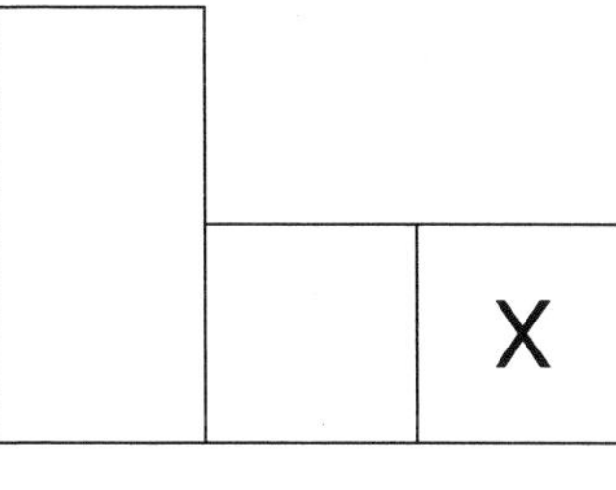

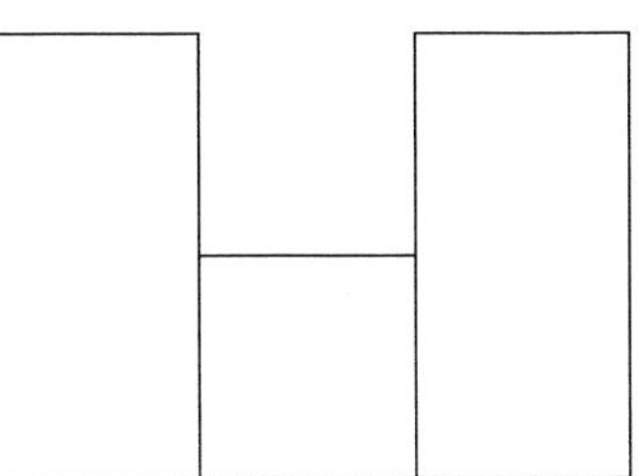

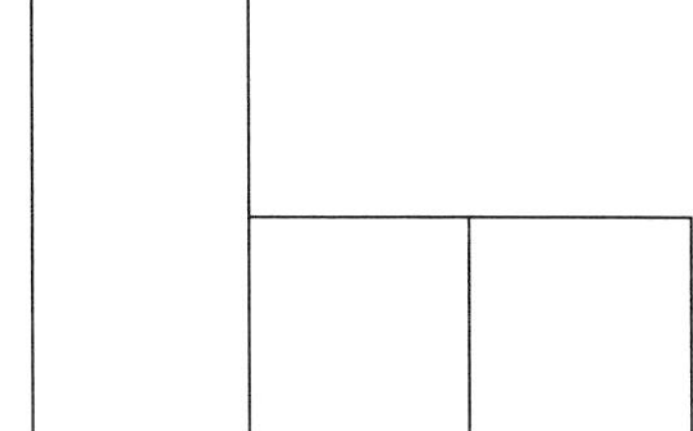

5. Which list words begin with "d"?

____ ____ ____ and ____ ____ ____

6. Match the pairs.

clubhouse

Word Chain

1. Collect strips of paper.
2. Write a spelling word on each strip.
3. Join to make a word chain.

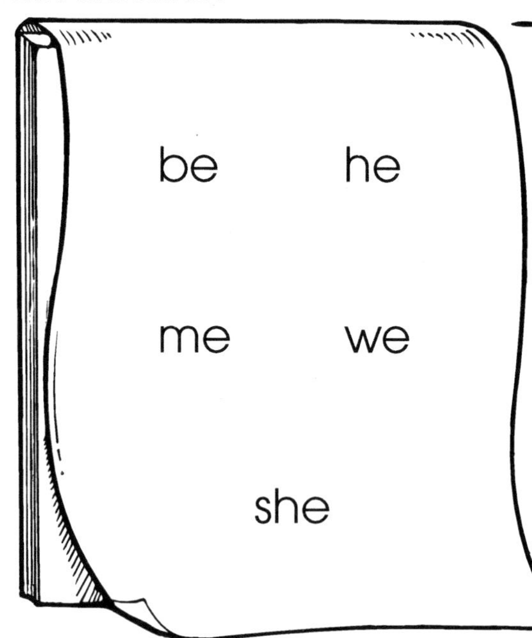

Look at the words.
Say each word slowly.

The "e" says ☐ on the end of each word.
Underline the "e" in each word.

1. Complete the list words.

sh _____

m _____

h _____

b _____

w _____

2. These list words are backwards. Write them correctly.

em _____ _____ ew _____ _____

eb _____ _____ eh _____ _____

ehs _____ _____ _____

3. Color the List Nineteen words.

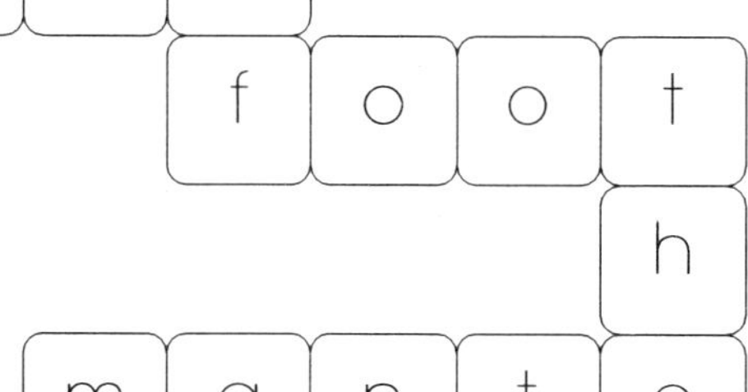

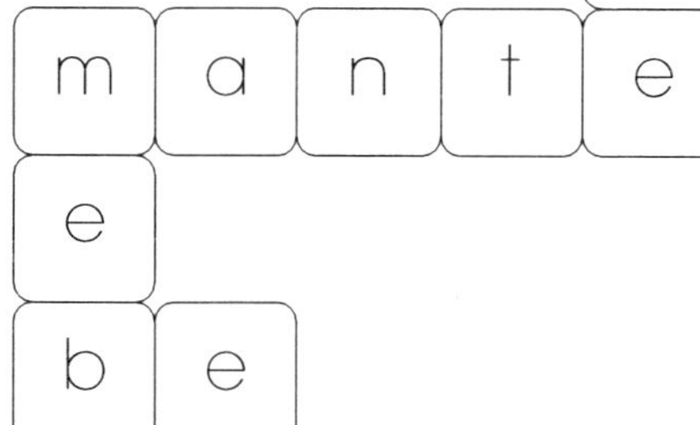

Your notebook

1. Write the **List Nineteen** words using – look, say, cover, write, check.
2. Write each **List Nineteen** word in a sentence.
3. Write each **My List** word using – look, cover, say, write, check.
4. Make word shapes for each **My List** word.

 www.worldteacherspress.com

4. Use the List Nineteen words to complete the sentences.

(a) __________ have a pet kitten.

(b) My kitten loves __________ .

(c) __________ has a new dress.

(d) __________ likes to ride his bike.

5. Which list word was not used? __________

8. Draw a word that sounds like "be."

6. Match each word to its picture.

see 

sea  

7. Circle the correct word.

by

bye

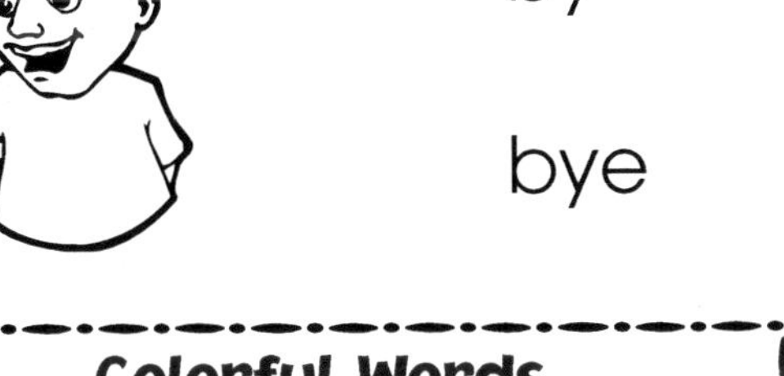

Colorful Words

1. Write the **List Nineteen** words, using your favorite color to show the pattern.
2. Write each **My List** word, using your favorite color to show the tricky part.

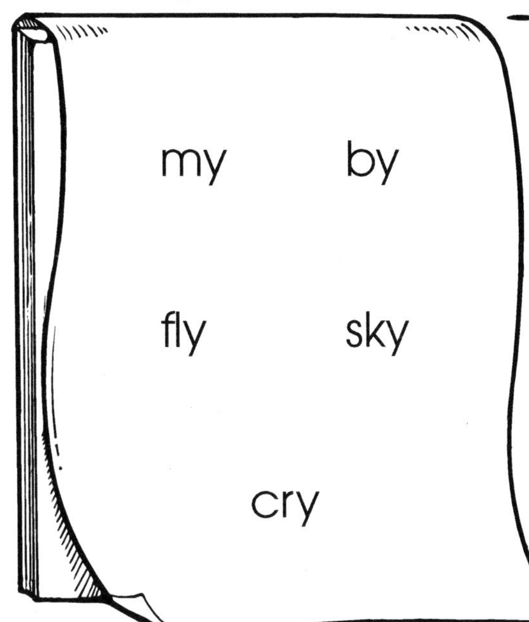

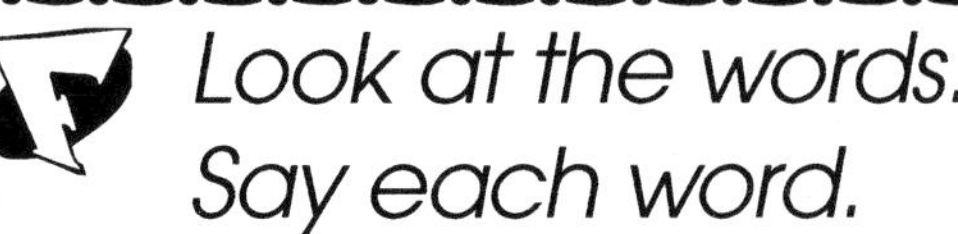

Look at the words.
Say each word.

The "y" says ☐ on the end of each word.
Underline the "y" in each word.

2. These list words are backwards. Write them correctly.

y r c ________________

y b ________________

y k s ________________

y m ________________

y l f ________________

1. Complete the list words.

b ______

cr ______

fl ______

m ______

sk ______

3. Circle the "y" words.

1. Write the **List Twenty** words using – look, say, cover, write, check.
2. Write each **List Twenty** word in a sentence.
3. Write each **My List** word using – look, say, cover, write, check.
4. Make word shapes for each **My List** word.

4. Use the List Twenty words to complete the sentences.

(a) Birds can ______________ in the ______________ .

(b) The bin is __________ the tree.

(c) __________ lunch box is green.

(d) A baby can ______________ .

5. Circle the "y" words. Draw the picture.

A bird and a plane are flying in the sky.

6. Add "ing" to these words.

fly______________

cry______________

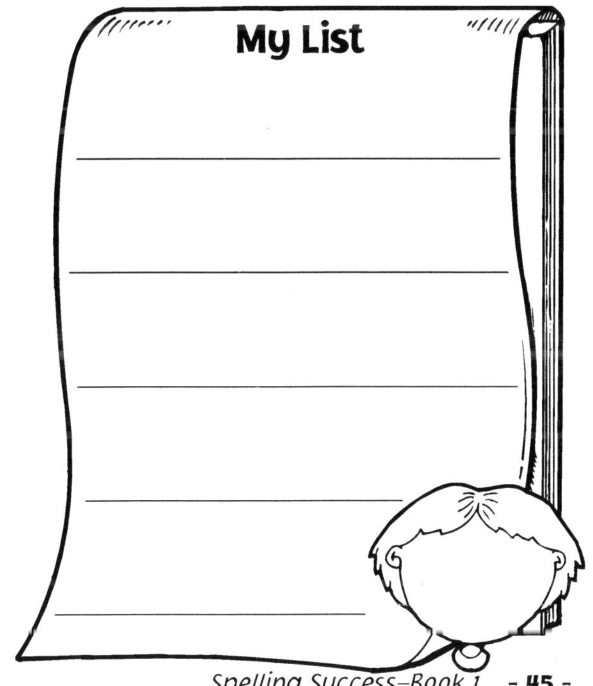

clubhouse

Make a Book

1. Use paper to make a book.
2. Write the words from both lists in the book, one on each page.
3. Draw a picture for each to show the word.

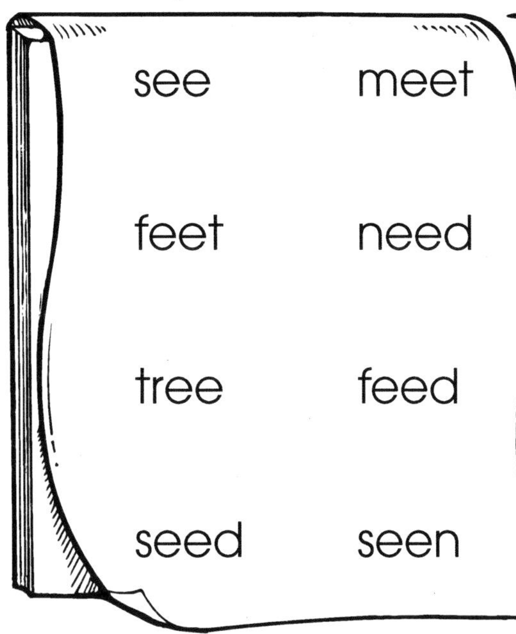

Look at the words.
Say each word.
Underline the pattern.

The pattern is ☐☐.

1. Complete the list words.

m ____ ____ t

tr ____ ____

s ____ ____

n ____ ____ d

f ____ ____ d

f ____ ____ t

s ____ ____ n

s ____ ____ d

2. These list words are backwards. Write them correctly.

d e e n ____________

t e e m ____________

t e e f ____________

3. Which list words rhyme with...

feet? ____________

need? ____________

____

see? ____________

Your notebook

1. Write the **List Twenty-One** words using – look, say, cover, write, check.
2. Choose five **List Twenty-One** words and write each in a sentence.
3. Write each **My List** word using – look, say, cover, write, check.
4. Make word shapes for each **My List** word.

4. Use the List Twenty-One words to complete the sentences.

   (a) Have you ______________________ my book?

   (b) Plant the ______________________ under the tree.

   (c) The nest is in the ______________________ .

   (d) You ______________________ a sharp pencil.

5. Which list word am I? Draw me.

   I have a trunk.
   Birds live in me.
   Cats climb up me.

   I am a ______________________ .

6. Name parts of your body with "ee" in them.

   f _____ _____ t   kn _____ _____

   t_____ _____ th

clubhouse

Accordion Words

1. Fold long strips of paper like an accordion.
2. Write the words from both lists on the strips.
3. Cut the strips at the end of each word.

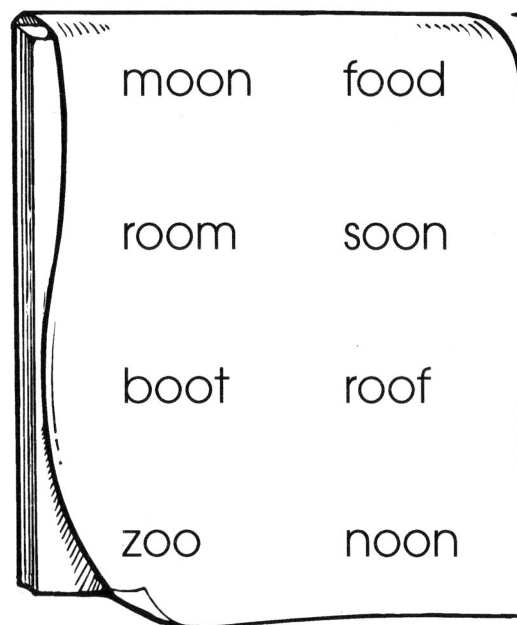

Look at the words.
Say each word.
Underline the pattern.

The pattern is ☐ ☐ .

2. These list words are backwards.
   Write them correctly.

d o o f ____________________

n o o s ____________________

f o o r ____________________

1. Complete the list words.

f ___ ___ d

s ___ ___ n

r ___ ___ f

z ___ ___

r ___ ___ m

n ___ ___ n

b ___ ___ t

m ___ ___ n

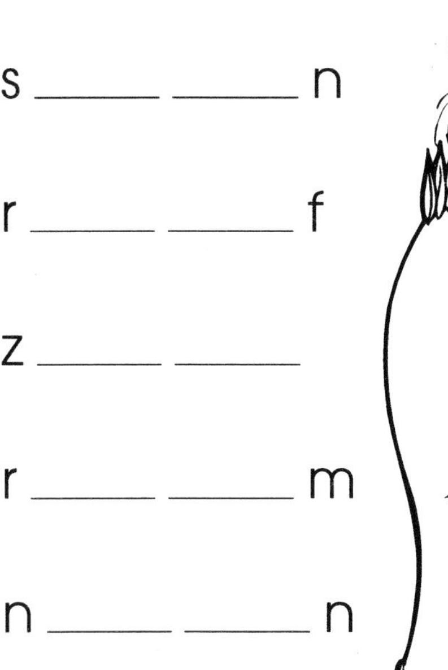

3. Which list word looks the same backwards and forwards?

____

4. Add "s" to these words.

zoo ____________________

moon ____________________

boot ____________________

room ____________________

your note-book

1. Write the **List Twenty-Two** words using – look, say, cover, write, check.
2. Choose five **List Twenty-Two** words and write each in a sentence.
3. Write each **My List** word using – look, say, cover, write, check.
4. Make word shapes for each **My List** word.

5. Use the List Twenty-Two words to complete the sentences.

(a) I eat my lunch at ______________________ .

(b) The ______________________ shines at night.

(c) Some animals live in a ______________________ .

(d) My cat likes to walk on the ______________________ .

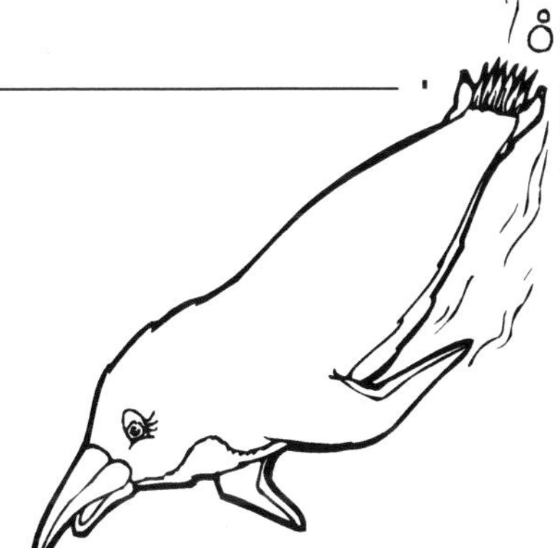

6. Match the words to their meaning.

food	A part of a house.
room	A type of shoe.
soon	Something we eat at mealtimes.
boot	In a short time.

7. On another piece of paper, draw your favorite room in your house.

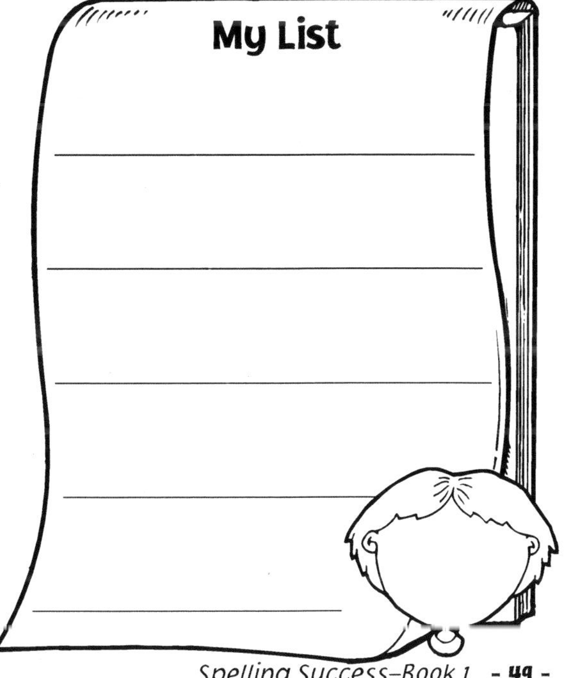

clubhouse

Finger Paint Your Words

Use paint to write the words from both lists with your finger.

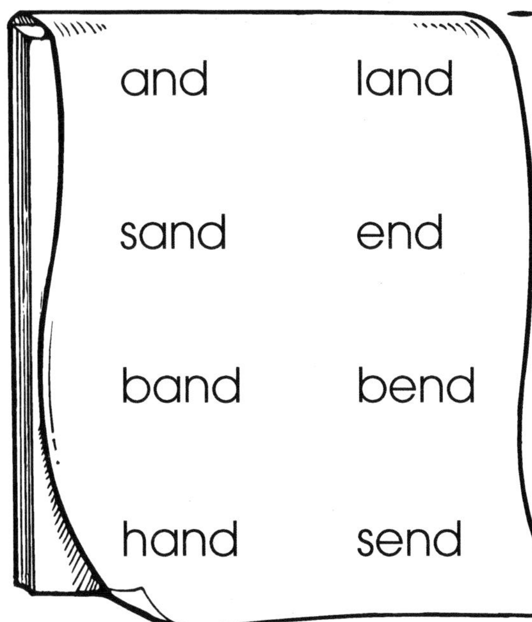

Look at the words.
Say each word.
Underline the patterns.
The patterns are

☐ ☐ ☐

and ☐ ☐ ☐ .

2. These list words are backwards.
   Write them correctly.

d n a l ________________

d n e ________________

d n a ________________

1. Complete the list words.

l ___ ___ ___

h ___ ___ ___

b ___ ___ ___

a ___ ___

s ___ ___ ___

e ___ ___

s ___ ___ ___

b ___ ___ ___

3. Which list words begin with...

b? ________________

____

s? ________________

____

Your note-book

1. Write the **List Twenty-Three** words using – look, say, cover, write, check.
2. Choose five **List Twenty-Three** words and write each in a sentence.
3. Write each **My List** word using – look, say, cover, write, check.
4. Make word shapes for each **My List** word.

4. Use the List Twenty-Three words to complete the sentences.

(a) Sam likes to eat spaghetti ________________ meatballs.

(b) I draw with my left ________________ .

(c) Can you ________________ your arm?

(d) The beach ________________ is hot.

5. Use the clues to fill in the missing list words.

Across

1. I will __________ a letter.

4. I + and = __________

Down

2. to finish

3. a group that plays music

6. On another piece of paper, write the parts of your body that can bend.

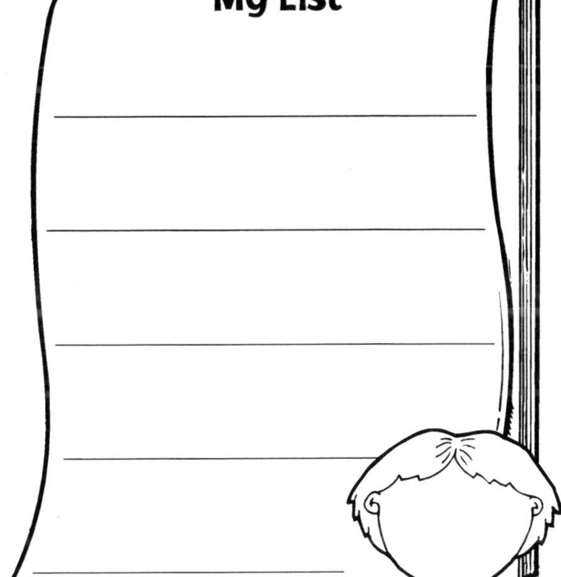

Pipe Cleaner Words

Use pipe cleaners to make the words from both lists.

and

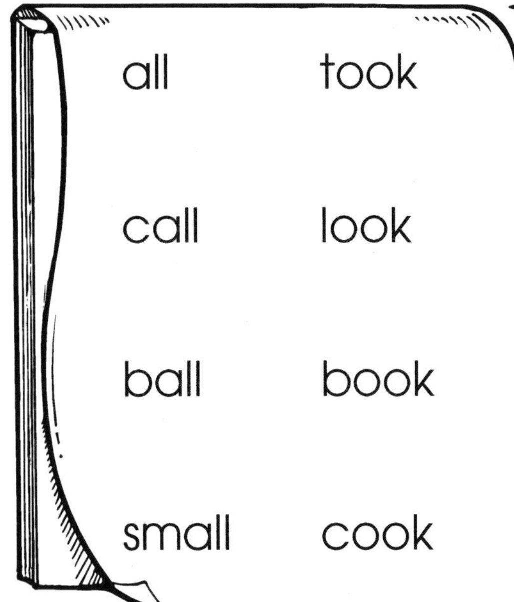

Look at the words.
Say each word.
Underline the patterns.
The patterns are

and ☐☐☐.

1. Complete the list words.

sm ___ ___ ___

t ___ ___ ___

___ ___ ___

c ___ ___ ___

c ___ ___ ___

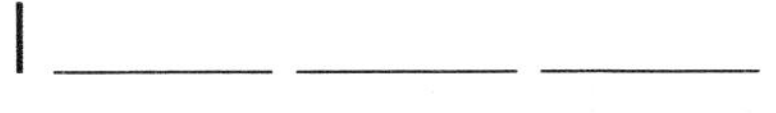

l ___ ___ ___

b ___ ___ ___

b ___ ___ ___

2. These list words are backwards. Write them correctly.

k o o l ______________

l l a m s ______________

l l a ______________

k o o t ______________

l l a c ______________

3. Add "s" to these words.

cook ______________

ball ______________

book ______________

Your note-book

1. Write the **List Twenty-Four** words using – look, say, cover, write, check.
2. Choose five **List Twenty-Four** words and write each in a sentence.
3. Write each **My List** list word using – look, say, cover, write, check.
4. Make word shapes for each **My List** word.

4. Use the List Twenty-Four words to complete the sentences.

   (a) Tim likes to ____________________ toast.

   (b) Please pick up ____________________ of your trash.

   (c) Fiona __________________ her book back to the library.

   (d) Don't ____________________ out in class.

5. Match the words to their meaning.

Word	Meaning
ball	Something you can read.
book	To use your eyes to see.
small	Something you can balance, kick or throw.
look	Not big.

6. On another piece of paper, draw the cover of your favorite book.

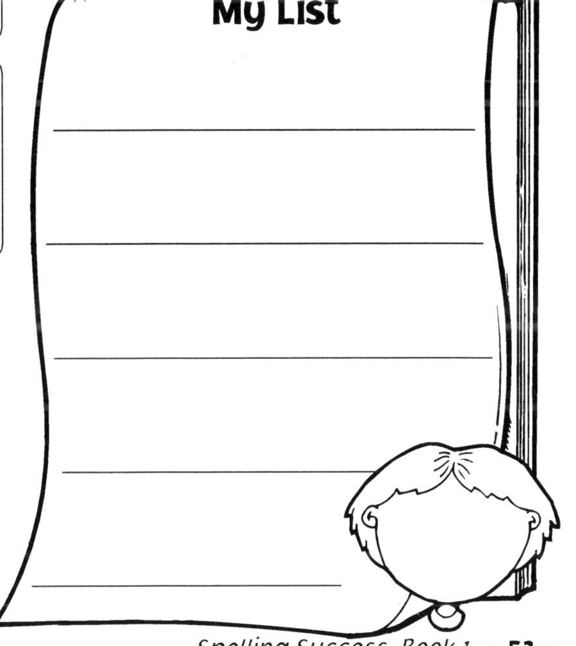

clubhouse

Make a Bookmark

1. Use thick cardboard to make a bookmark.
2. Write the words from each list on the bookmark.
3. Decorate your bookmark.

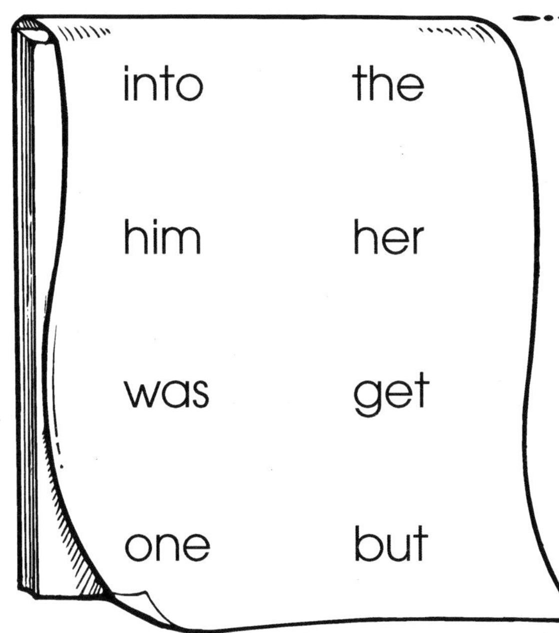

Look at the words.
Say each word slowly.
Underline the tricky part.

1. Complete the list words.
   Fill in the missing vowels.

h r

____ n ____

th ____

w ____ s

b ____ t

____ nt ____

h ____ m

g ____ t

2. Choose a list word to rhyme with each of these words.

wet ____________________

shut ____________________

do ____________________

dim ____________________

sun ____________________

fur ____________________

3. Which list words didn't you use?

____

____

Your notebook

1. Write the **List Twenty-Five** words using – look, say, cover, write, check.
2. Choose five **List Twenty-Five** words and write each in a sentence.
3. Write each **My List** word using – look, say, cover, write, check.
4. Make word shapes for each **My List** word.

4. Choose the correct word from List Twenty-Five.

(a) (But, Him, The) ______________ dog likes to bark.

(b) Put your trash (her, into, get) ______________ the bin.

(c) Zoe (her, was, the) ______________ late for school.

(d) William wanted to play outside (him, one, but) ______________ it was raining.

5. Finish the crossword puzzle using the letters below.

6. Draw something you would like to **get** as a present on another piece of paper.

clubhouse

Word Sort

1. Sort the **List Twenty-Five** words from the easiest to the hardest.
2. Talk about your choice with a friend.
3. Sort the **My List** words in the same way.

Lists One to Ten - Pages 16-25
Teacher check

List Eleven - Page 26
1. Teacher check
2. **can**, fan, man, ran, pan
3. Teacher check
4. Teacher check

Page 27
5. can, man, fan
6. Teacher check
7. pan, ran, can, man, fan

List Twelve - Page 28
1. Teacher check
2. met
3. vet, pet, net, wet, met
4. **vet**, met, net, wet, pet
5. Teacher check

Page 29
6. net, vet, wet
7. Teacher check
8. pet, net, vet, met, wet

List Thirteen - Page 30
1. Teacher check
2. **win**, fin, pin, tin, bin
3. win, fin, bin, pin, tin
4. Teacher check

Page 31
5. fin, pin, bin
6. Teacher check
7. bin, tin, win, fin, pin

List Fourteen - Page 32
1. Teacher check
2. **cot**, hot, dot, tot, pot
3. cot, dot, tot, pot, hot
4. Teacher check

Page 33
5. cot, tot, pot
6. Teacher check
7. tot, pot, dot, cot, hot

List Fifteen - Page 34
1. Teacher check
2. **hug**, rug, jug, mug, bug
3. jug, hug, rug, bug, mug
4. Teacher check

Page 35
5. bug, rug, jug
6. Teacher check
7. rug, mug, hug, jug, bug

List Sixteen - Page 36
1. **has,** ten, big, dog, nut
2. dog, ten, big, nut, has
3. dog, ten, has, big, nut

Page 37
4. has, **b**ig, **n**ut, dog, ten
5. Teacher check
6. dog, big

List Seventeen - Page 38
1. **had,** yes, did, got, bus
2. had, yes, did, got, bus
3. yes, got, had, bus, did

Page 39
4. yes, bus, **d**id, had, got
5. had, did
6. Answers may vary

List Eighteen - Page 40
1. **Dad,** bed, dig, box, Mom
2. Dad, bed, dig, box, Mom
3. bed, box, Dad, Mom, dig

Page 41
4. dig, Dad, box, bed, Mom
5. Dad, dig
6. Mom-Dad, girl-boy, queen-king, princess-prince

List Nineteen - Page 42
1. Teacher check
2. me, we, be, he, she
3. Teacher check

Page 43
4. **(a)** We **(b)** me **(c)** She **(d)** He
5. be
6. Teacher check
7. bye
8. Teacher check

List Twenty - Page 44
1. Teacher check
2. cry, by, sky, my, fly
3. Teacher check

Page 45
4. **(a)** fly, sky **(b)** by **(c)** My **(d)** cry
5. Teacher check
6. flying, crying

List Twenty-One - Page 46
1. Teacher check
2. need, meet, feet
3. feet - meet; need - feed, seed; see-tree

Page 47
4. **(a)** seen **(b)** seed **(c)** tree **(d)** need
5. tree
6. feet, knee, teeth

List Twenty-Two - Page 48
1. Teacher check
2. food, soon, roof
3. noon
4. zoos, moons, boots, rooms

Page 49
5. **(a)** noon **(b)** moon **(c)** zoo **(d)** roof
6. Teacher check
7. Teacher check

List Twenty-Three - Page 50
1. Teacher check
2. land, end, and
3. b-band, bend; s-sand, send

Page 51
4. **(a)** and **(b)** hand **(c)** bend **(d)** sand
5. **across** 1. send 4. land **down** 2. end 3. band
6. Teacher check

List Twenty-Four - Page 52
1. Teacher check
2. look, small, all, took, call
3. cooks, balls, books

Page 53
4. **(a)** cook **(b)** all **(c)** took **(d)** call
5. Teacher check
6. Teacher check

List Twenty-Five - Page 54
1. Teacher check
2. get, but, into, him, one, her
3. the, was

Page 55
4. **(a)** The **(b)** into **(c)** was **(d)** but
5. him, one, into, get
6. Teacher check

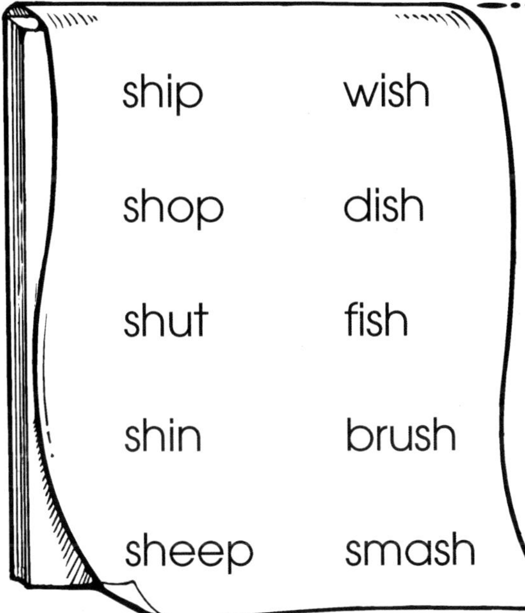

Look at the words.
Say each word.
Underline the pattern.

The pattern is ☐☐ *at the beginning or end of each word.*

1. **Fill in the missing vowels to complete the list words.**

sh ____ ____ p

w ____ sh

br ____ sh

sh ____ t

sh ____ p

d ____ sh

f ____ sh

sm ____ sh

sh ____ n

sh ____ p

2. **Word Hunt**

Which list words rhyme?

____

____

____

Which list words have five letters?

____

____

____

Which list words have four letters and end in "p"?

____________________ ____________________

1. Write the **List One** words using – look, say, cover, write, check.
2. Write five more **sh** words. Check the spelling.
3. Write **My List** words using – look, say, cover, write, check.
4. Find small words in **My List** words.

3. Find small words in these List One words.

ship ______ shop ______ shut ______

shin ______ sheep ______ ______

4. Use the List One words to complete the sentences.

(a) Please ______ the door.

(b) A baby ______ is a lamb.

(c) A ______ lives in water.

(d) He sailed across the ocean on a ______ .

5. Add "s" to these words to make them say more than one.

ship ______ shop ______

shin ______

6. Add "es" to these words to make them say more than one.

wish ______

dish ______

brush ______

clubhouse

Make a Book

1. Use paper to make a book.
2. Write a word from both lists on each page until all words have been used.
3. Draw a picture for each.

My List

______

______

______

______

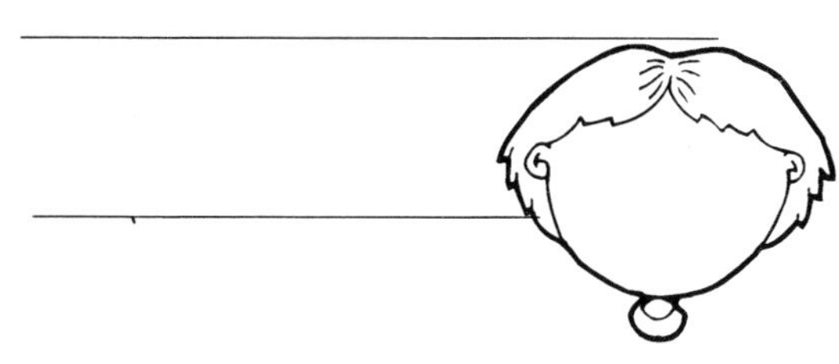

List Two **Spelling Success**

chop	rich
chip	such
chin	each
chick	lunch
chest	much

Look at the words.
Say each word.
Underline the pattern.

The pattern is ☐☐ *at the beginning or end of each word.*

2. Unjumble the list words.

poch ____________________

icrh ____________________

humc ____________________

ucsh ____________________

chea ____________________

pich ____________________

1. Fill in the missing vowels to complete the list words.

___ ___ ch	ch ___ st
ch ___ p	s ___ ch
r ___ ch	ch ___ n
ch ___ ck	l ___ nch
m ___ ch	ch ___ p

3. Guess the list word by its shape.

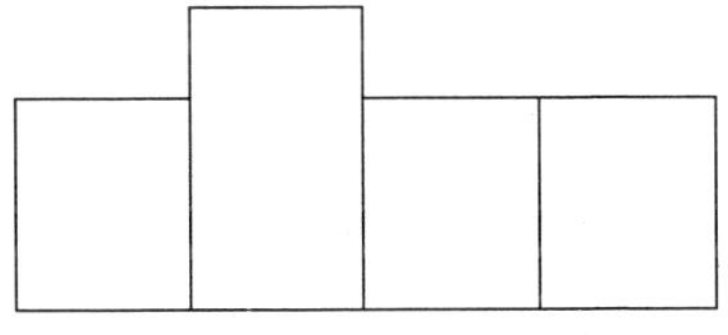

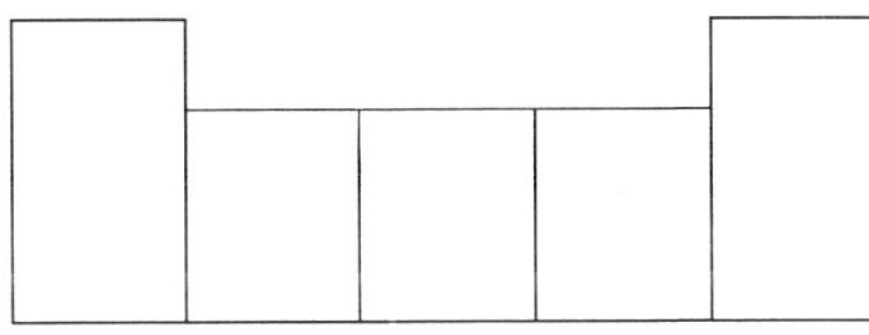

1. Write the **List Two** words using – look, say, cover, write, check.
2. Write five more **ch** words. Check the spelling.
3. Write **My List** words using – look, say, cover, write, check.
4. Make word shapes for each **My List** word.

4. Use the List Two words to complete the sentences.

   (a) It was ________________ a hot day.

   (b) Give a book to ________________ child.

   (c) How ________________ does it cost?

5. Look at each picture. Circle the correct word. Write it on the line.

chick, chicks ________________

________________ lunch, lunches

chest, chests ________________

6. Find small words in these List Two words.

   chop ________________

   chip ________________

   chin ________________

My List

____

____

____

____

clubhouse

Pipe Cleaner Words

Use pipe cleaners to make the words from both lists.

List Three **Spelling Success**

gave	like
take	ride
make	kite
made	five
came	time

Look at the words.
Say each word.
Underline the patterns.

The patterns are ☐ – ☐ *and* ☐ – ☐.

The "e" makes the vowel sound long.

1. Write "a–e" or "i–e" to complete the list words.

m ____ d ____ k ____ t ____

t ____ m ____ g ____ v ____

c ____ m ____ m ____ k ____

l ____ k ____ r ____ d ____

f ____ v ____ t ____ k ____

2. Write a list word that rhymes with these.

game ____________

bike ____________

hive ____________

save ____________

shade ____________

3. What am I?

I can fly.
I don't have wings.
I have a long string
and a tail.

I am a ____________ .

1. Write the **List Three** words using – look, say, cover, write, check.
2. Choose five list words and write each in a sentence.
3. Write **My List** words using – look, say, cover, write, check.
4. Write a rhyming word for each **My List** word.

4. Unjumble the sentences. Circle the List Three words.

(a) you. Take with book the

____

(b) bike? you ride Can a

____

(c) is What time? the

____

(d) can bed. my I make

____

"e" goes away
when "ing" comes to stay.
For example, take – taking.

5. Add "ing" to these list words.

make ______________

ride ______________

time ______________

My List

____

____

____

____

clubhouse

Accordion Words

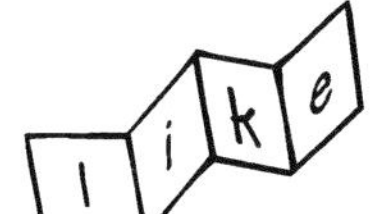

1. Fold long strips of paper like an accordion.
2. Write the words from both lists on the strips.
3. Cut the strip at the end of each word.

This is a fi ___ tree.

A fig tr ___ ___ has f ___ ___ s on it.

Can you s ___ ___ the figs?

Draw a big pot of fig jam.

Figs are good for you.

They have lots of seeds in them.

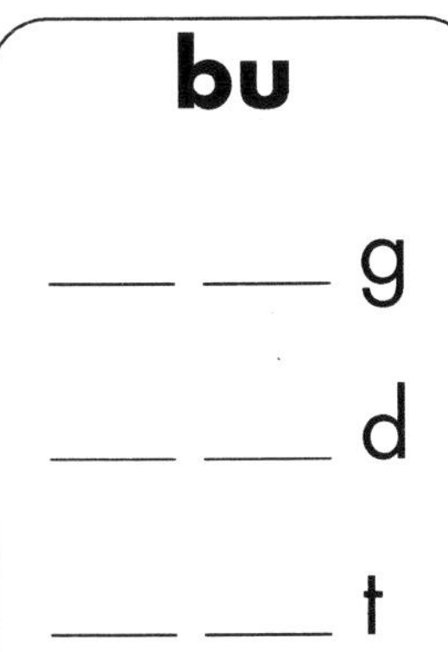

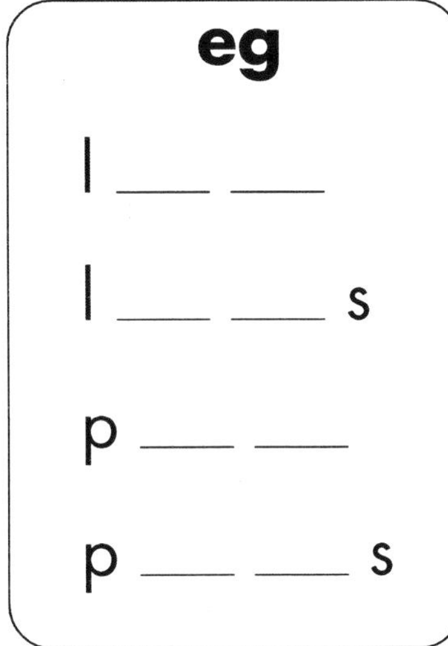

This is a b ___ ___ .

Bugs have six l ___ ___ s.

This bug sits on a b ___ d.

It e ___ ___ s the bud.

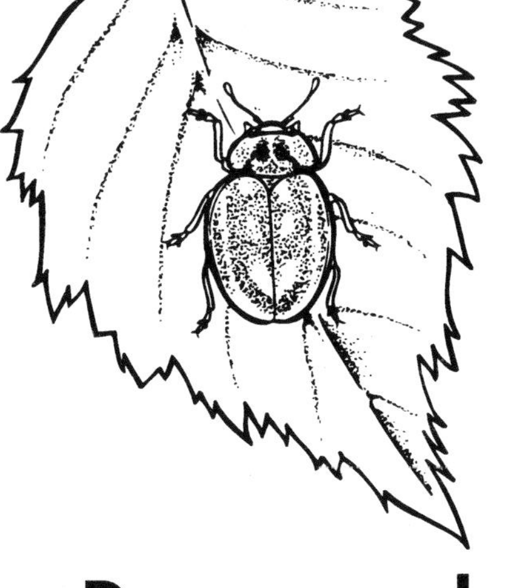

Draw a red bug on a green leaf.

Ladybugs are good for the garden.

They eat bugs that eat the plants.

